KNUCKLEHEADS IN THE NEWS

KNUCKLEHEADS IN THE NEWS

JOHN "KATO" MACHAY

With an introduction by
Scott Shannon and Todd Pettengill

BALLANTINE BOOKS

NEW YORK

Copyright © 1996 by John Machay

All rights reserved under International and Pan-American Copyright Conventions. Published in the United States by Ballantine Books, a division of Random House, Inc., New York, and simultaneously in Canada by Random House of Canada Limited, Toronto.

Interior design by Michaelis/Carpelis Design Assoc.

http://www.randomhouse.com

Library of Congress Catalog Card Number: 96-96851

ISBN: 345-40988-4

Cover design by David Stevenson
Cover photo © Carl Fischer

Manufactured in the United States of America

First Edition: September 1996

10 9 8 7 6 5 4 3 2 1

DEDICATION

To Jill, Bobby, and Gabrielle, for continually finding new diversions during the endless hours I spent locked away in my office and for putting up with the stacks of newspaper clippings scattered throughout the house...

...and in memory of Joseph Livorsi, whose love will live on for generations to come....

ACKNOWLEDGMENTS

A plethora of grats to the following for their encouragement and support: Scott Shannon, Todd Pettengill, Tom Cuddy, Mitch Dolan, Naomi DiClemente, Joe Nolan, Diana "Lady Di" Ferrito, Joe "Monkey Boy" Pardavilla, Chris Basil, Cathy Repetti, Ellen Archer, Ling Lucas, Ed Vesneske Jr., Brian Alcorn, Jacquie Clifton, Nancy Lupo, and Barbara Hackett.

TABLE OF CONTENTS

INTRODUCTION

By Scott Shannon and Todd Pettengill

In this world there are people who will tell you it isn't *what* you know, it's *who* you know that gets you to the top of your chosen profession. Other people say it isn't *who* you know, it's *what* you know that counts.

In the communications business it isn't *what* you know or *who* you know, it's *when* you know what you know before who-knows-who knows you know what you know.

Kato ought to know. Ever since we found him standing outside Manhattan's Lincoln Tunnel and persuaded him to trade in his squeegee for a clipboard, he's never ceased to amaze us with his omnipotent power to track down the most bizarre stories in places you don't even want to know about. Stories about unusual people reacting to normal situations. Stories about normal people reacting to unusual situations. Unusual stories about reactive people in *any* type of situation. In short, stories about Knuckleheads.

What is it that makes John "Kato" Machay a George Michael in a world of Andrew Ridgleys? Easy. Kato *himself* is a Knucklehead. And like the man says, it takes one to know one.

Now you ask, "What makes the executive producer of *Billboard* magazine's number-one morning show in America a *Knucklehead*?" It isn't the sleepless nights he's spent trying to figure out why all seven dwarfs share the same run-down shack when they mine diamonds for a living; it's not because he's seen every episode of *Mama's Family* 623 times apiece; it isn't even his lengthy chats with the ghost of Eleanor Roosevelt on the roof of the Ballantine Publishing building. The fact is, we're *all* Knuckleheads at one time or another.

Which probably explains why "Knuckleheads in the News" continues to be one of the most popular features on our show. For each time you've lost your car keys, there's always some whacked-out bonehead who's lost his car; for the times you accidentally swallowed your Bubble Yum, there are half-wits who've swallowed toothbrushes, gear shift knobs, and golf balls; for every one of life's mishaps that make you end up feeling stupid, there's always someone *stupider*. We realize all this is nothing but a load of psychological horse crap, but it sure looks good in print.

So, in view of the laughter they've brought into our lives—and because we figure it's a good idea to kiss a little ass if we want to avoid any lawsuits—we salute the embarrassed people of the world who've earned the distinguished honor of being selected for "Knuckleheads in the News."

We could go on and on—in fact, we *have* gone on and on—but it's time to coax Kato out of the supply closet. He's been in there for the past three hours trying to figure out why, if one dwarf is a "doc," he doesn't do something for Sneezy.

KNUCKLEHEADS
IN THE NEWS

CHAPTER I

KNUCKLEHEADS ON WHEELS

We all lose our patience with slow-moving drivers at one time or another, but a sluggish sedan in Tustin, California, apparently caused a twenty-six-year-old woman to lose her *mind*.

Lisa Lind was cruising along a two-lane canyon road when she came upon a lethargic motorist leisurely driving in front of her pickup. Unable to pass due to the winding road's limited visibility, Lind honked her horn in hopes of getting the driver to move over to the shoulder. When that didn't work, she tried flashing her brights.

The driver *still* didn't respond, so Lind took the next obvious course of action: She rammed her truck into the car's rear end a couple of times. Despite her glaring cries for attention, the car continued to tool along at the same steady pace.

Forgetting her original mission to simply pass the car, Lind drove into the left lane, pulled up alongside the listless vehicle and began swinging at it with a baseball bat. Maneuvering along the winding road while leaning across the seat with a Louisville Slugger in her hand proved too much for the woman, and she ended up denting the door of her own truck.

Needless to say, the self-inflicted damage brought Lind's animosity to a feverish peak, so she grabbed a can of air freshener and threw it at the car, breaking one of its windows. Apparently satisfied, Lind sped up, veered back into the right lane and continued on her journey.

The other driver had little trouble remembering the ironic message on Lind's customized license plate when reporting the incident to police. It read PEACE 95.

After charging the woman with assault, the arresting officer said, "She said she got the license plate because she thought there was too much violence going on in today's society."

━━━━

In Rome, a motorist who was stuck in traffic came up with a surefire way to keep his plane grounded as he made his way to the airport: He picked up his mobile phone and called in a phony bomb threat.

Unfortunately, the man ended up missing his flight anyway. Although the aircraft was still waiting at the gate when the traveler arrived, so were several police officers, who arrested him.

━━━━

Police in Natchitoches, Louisiana, arrested Simpson Williams Jr. after he rammed his Mercedes into a patrol car.

When questioned by authorities, Williams said he attacked the Chevrolet police cruiser because his German car told him to "kill" an American-made vehicle.

━━━━━━━

Some of the best "Knuckleheads Behind the Wheel" stories never even make it to print. If the responding officer fails to file a report, a potentially entertaining incident can become little more than precinct chatter.

Case in point: A Stamford police officer—who requested anonymity—likes to amuse friends and colleagues with the story of a fifty-five-year-old woman identified only as "Sharon." In early 1994 she was involved in an accident that involved thirteen vehicles, six light poles, and a traffic sign—and she escaped without a scratch.

The minor catastrophe occurred between one and two A.M., when Sharon attempted to back out of a parking stall at a local bar. While trying to accomplish the customarily simple maneuver, she smashed the rear bumper of her Toyota Celica into another parked car, breaking its taillight. Panicked, she threw her coupe into drive and stepped on the gas, barreling right into *another* stationary car. The impact caused it to bound forward and strike a third car, which rammed a fourth.

"The parking lot was pretty full," the cop said. "After running into the first couple of cars, she got real overwhelmed."

Sharon was *so* overwhelmed, in fact, she didn't see the light pole to the left of her first mechanical victim. She hit it so hard, it fell over, crushing the roof of a *fifth* car.

Apparently wanting to leave no witnesses, Sharon immediately went to work on the other poles that supported the row of lights. She hit a second while trying to steer around the first downed pole, clocked a third when she attempted to turn away from the second, and knocked a fourth onto the sixth car when she misjudged the distance between the last pole and the thoroughfare.

Turning onto the street, Sharon nailed a car that was parked on the shoulder. The seventh car hit the eighth car, which knocked down the stop sign.

In an attempt to regain her composure, the disoriented woman pulled onto what she thought was the shoulder—in actuality, somebody's front lawn—and slammed into a fire hydrant. She sideswiped a fifth light pole while driving back onto the road.

The conflict with pole number five caused Sharon to drive all the way across the road, bulldoze through a fence, and bash into a gazebo. There, the unsettled Celica finally found a resting place—in a flower bed.

Surprisingly, the results of her Breathalyzer test showed she *wasn't* drunk. Even more surprisingly, she wasn't charged or ticketed—which probably explains the police officer's request to be anonymous.

From the "likely story" department: Police in Toronto, Canada, arrested a sixty-year-old man on charges of drunk driving after he smashed into a patrol car that was parked in front of a local police station.

When questioned by authorities, the man said he had driven to the station to see if he was "sober enough to drive."

———

When it comes to domestic disputes, most relationship experts agree it's best to give the other party some time to cool off before sitting down to talk things out.

That's exactly what a man in Redwood City, California, tried to do after getting into an argument with his girlfriend. Unfortunately, his disenchanted steady didn't want any part of it.

By the time the Redwood City Police Department got involved, twenty-three-year-old Frank Bamba was speeding down a busy highway—with his girlfriend clinging to the roof of his van.

According to police reports, Bamba tried to end a nasty lover's quarrel by climbing into his van and driving away. His girlfriend—whose name wasn't released—wasn't quite ready to give up the fight, however. Unable to convince Bamba to stick around so they could resolve the spat, she did the next best thing: She mounted the rear bumper as he sped off.

Refusing to concede, the disenchanted Bamba kept right on driving. When he turned onto a major highway, his girlfriend somehow managed to scale the van's rear and grab ahold of the luggage rack on the roof.

Police said Bamba drove for more than an hour before he was finally pulled over.

———

As a patrol officer working the weekend graveyard shift in the Bronx, Barbara Daquino thought she'd seen it all. But that was before a blue Oldsmobile sped past her parked police cruiser one Saturday night.

Even if thirty-one-year-old Kenneth Cousens hadn't been weaving all over the road, Daquino wouldn't have had any trouble determining something was wrong. As Cousens recklessly made his way down Boston Post Road, Daquino was blinded by two torrents of blazing sparks gushing from the sedan's rear end.

Struggling to make out the car's license plate amid the deluge of impromptu fireworks, Daquino flipped on the red-and-blues and succeeded in getting the New York man to pull over. An inspection of the Oldsmobile quickly unveiled the reason for the sparks: Cousens was driving with no back tires. Just rims.

Cousens—who was arrested and charged with driving while intoxicated—said he had no idea what happened to the tires.

———

POLICE BEGIN CAMPAIGN TO RUN DOWN JAYWALKERS

If you ever happen to visit Moonachie, New Jersey, there are three simple rules you'll need to follow: (1) Don't mispronounce the town's name (it's "Moon-OCK-ee"); (2) If you're a hockey fan, don't walk the streets wearing a New York Rangers T-shirt (residents take great pride in the New Jersey Devils); and

(3) Don't mess with the Moonachie Police Department—even if you're a firefighter.

Firefighter Wally Peterson, from nearby South Hackensack, found out about rule number three the hard way.

When someone called the fire department to report diesel fumes, Peterson jumped into his fire engine, flipped on the siren, and sped off. Because South Hackensack is divided into three noncontiguous sections, Peterson's route took him through neighboring Moonachie, a common occurrence for South Hackensack police and fire officials.

After attending to the emergency, the volunteer firefighter returned to his truck, where he found Moonachie Police Sgt. John Rossillo and another officer waiting for him—not to offer praise for a job well done, but to write Peterson a speeding ticket.

"Here we're talking about a volunteer doing his job . . . and he gets a ticket," a South Hackensack official complained to the press.

Despite a public outcry fueled by press reports, Moonachie police officials stood behind Rossillo's decision.

"They just felt the driving was too reckless to ignore," Chief Michael McGahn said. "When they got to the scene, they let the firefighter do his job, and then asked for his license and registration."

═══════

Gung Chamsoo is lucky to be alive after one of his relatives drove a Honda over him. Twice.

The accident occurred on a sunny Sunday afternoon in September 1995 when Chamsoo was visiting another relative in Fosterdale, New York. Feeling restless, the forty-five-year-old Flushing resident decided to work on his manly figure by doing some exercises on the front lawn. Afterward, Chamsoo relaxed by stretching out in the grass.

Meanwhile, Kyung Chan Lee of Cochecton, New York, had just finished washing his 1989 Honda, which was parked in the driveway. He put the hose and bucket away and climbed into the car to drive to church.

But instead of navigating the four-door sedan down the driveway, Lee somehow managed to back onto the lawn, where he drove right over Chamsoo's chest.

"I heard a big scream," Lee said. "It scared me, so I pulled forward. I drive forward again over him."

Lee, thirty-four, added he didn't see his unlucky relative because he was wearing green, which caused him to "blend with the grass."

Amazingly, Chamsoo's injuries were minor. He was taken to Community General Hospital in Harris, New York, where he was treated and released.

Apparently, there were no hard feelings between the two men. After being released from the hospital, Chamsoo let Lee drive him home.

A man driving along a roadway in Edmonton, Alberta, Canada, nearly killed himself and three family members when he fainted behind the wheel.

According to police reports, the unpiloted vehicle crashed into another car and skidded into a utility pole before coming to a stop. Luckily, no one was injured.

Apparently, the man became ill and lost consciousness while listening to his son describe how the dentist removed his wisdom teeth earlier that day.

═══════════

At first, Jeffrey Telep thought he was watching a flaming comet grazing the earth's surface.

But after studying the radiant fireball for a few moments, the police officer soon realized the speeding object had four wheels, an antenna, and New Jersey license plates. It was a car, giving a whole new meaning to "burning up the road."

Telep was patrolling Route 46 in Lodi, New Jersey, when a Chevy Baretta—almost completely engulfed in flames—lit up the night as it came thundering down an eastbound lane. Telep expected the car to either stop or crash, but it kept traveling along the route to Manhattan as if there was nothing wrong.

Finally, Telep turned on his siren and lights to get the driver to stop the Burning Baretta. Even then the motorist continued to sit in the front seat, patiently waiting for Telep to approach the vehicle.

Lodi Police Detective Vincent Quatrone said Telep caught a "strong odor of alcohol" when the driver—identified as Milton M. Rodriguez-Menese—rolled down the window. As the fire continued to rage, Telep coaxed Rodriguez-Menese out of the kiln-on-wheels and submitted him to a Breathalyzer test. The oblivious motorist blew a 0.12, surpassing New Jersey's blood-alcohol limit of 0.10.

After the fire was extinguished, Rodriguez-Menese was arrested and booked on charges of driving while intoxicated. When he was released on his own recognizance the following day, he was shocked to learn his car had been torched.

"He apparently didn't even know his car was on fire," Quatrone said.

═══════

On May 19, 1996, a peaceful Sunday morning in Yorba Linda, California, was shattered when a reckless Jeep Cherokee came roaring through town.

Responding to a deluge of complaints, Yorba Linda police immediately got on the case and caught up with the speeding vehicle. The Jeep's driver—apparently no novice behind the wheel—wasn't about to be captured, however. The motorist eluded the exasperated patrolmen for thirty-two miles, leading them on a 90-mile-per-hour chase along several freeways. Finally, the early morning excitement came to an end when the Cherokee crashed into the side of an apartment building.

The officers cautiously approached the disabled vehicle, where they came face-to-face with the evasive culprit who'd managed to stay one step ahead of the long arm of justice. It was a twelve-year-old girl.

Before being taken to a juvenile detention facility, the seventh grader told police she had taken her parents' Jeep without permission and didn't pull over because she was afraid of getting into trouble.

———————

In Carrollton, Georgia, a Carroll County patrolman ordered the driver of a pickup to pull over after he clocked the vehicle doing 85 miles per hour.

When the cop asked for a driver's license and proof of registration, the motorist instead produced an ID card that many politicians refer to as a "get out of jail free card"—a diplomat identification credential, guaranteeing him immunity from annoyances like speeding tickets and other penalties one normally receives after breaking the law.

Although the ID listed the man as Khotu Bomani Kambui, a diplomat from the African nation of Nigritia, the officer had as much trouble swallowing the story as Mama Cass Elliot had swallowing her ham sandwich. Not only did Kambui have three shady-looking characters in the truck with him, the card itself didn't seem credible—it appeared as if it were hastily thrown together, complete with a Polaroid shot of Kambui glued next to his name.

When the distrusting cop questioned the amateurish paste-up job on such an important document, Kambui explained Nigritia was a poor country and that was all they could afford.

It wasn't the shoddy ID that confirmed the officer's suspicions, though. A quick call to the station house revealed *there was no Nigritia* in Africa—or anywhere else in the world, for that matter.

A search of the truck revealed several items that aren't generally considered standard supplies for a visiting diplomat: four handguns, a shotgun, two bags of marijuana, and a set of scales.

Kambui was arrested and booked on a variety of charges, including drug possession and carrying concealed weapons.

━━━━━

It wasn't exactly like the high-speed chases he saw in the movies, but a thirteen-year-old boy in North Carolina *still* had the ride of his life when he hijacked an empty school bus in January 1996.

Details on *how* the youth stole the bus are sketchy, but one thing's for sure: When Tabor City police caught up with him, he led them on a chase worthy of the *Smokey and the Bandit* trilogy.

Public school buses in North Carolina are equipped with mechanical speed limiters that restrict them to 46 miles per hour, but the hindrance didn't faze the unruly lad. Keeping the gas pedal pressed to the floor, he tried to run several patrol cars off the road as a veritable caravan followed him for ninety miles through the state.

The chase finally ended when the boy turned into a driveway at a high school in Shallotte, about thirty miles southeast of Tabor City. Seeing that the gate was closed, the underage thief put the bus in park, turned off the ignition, and set the emergency brake. Then he opened the door and bounded off the bus as innocently as if he were simply returning home from school.

"When he came off that bus, he was smiling and laughing," Tabor City Police Officer L. D. James said.

No criminal charges were filed, but the junior high school student was issued "several" traffic citations and released to the custody of his parents.

"We went forty-six miles per hour the whole time," James said. "But I'll tell you, that boy could drive that thing. He was crazy."

═══════

In Jefferson County, Missouri, police arrested nineteen-year-old David Zaricor after he crashed his car into another vehicle, killing a seventy-year-old woman.

According to records kept by the Missouri Highway Patrol, Zaricor told a trooper he lost control of his car when his girlfriend accidentally bit him while administering oral sex.

═══════

If there's one common complaint among police officers in the United States, it's that they're underappreciated. After subjecting themselves to grueling training sessions and arduous tests to make certain they're up to par, the country's finest take to the streets, working odd hours and putting their lives on the line—all in the interest of law and order.

Still, most average Joes view cops as nuisances: power-hungry bullies who park behind bushes waiting to ticket some poor sap who's frantically trying to make it to work on time. That is, until that poor sap gets his wallet stolen.

Indeed, there's a plethora of skills required to accurately enforce the law: One must be educated on local laws; one must know how to handle a gun; one must learn to stay calm in tense situations—the list goes on and on. But probably the greatest—and most overlooked—trait found in police officers is their ability to write legibly in the little boxes and blanks on police reports.

Anyone who's ever had to fill out an accident report can sympathize. In a space barely big enough to sign your name, you're expected to give a complete summary of your collision. Although most police forms instruct the person filing the report to keep the story brief and to the point, most people find that editing thoughts while transcribing them to paper isn't as easy as it sounds.

Here's some selected lines gathered from police reports from various parts of the country:

- Coming home, I drove into the wrong house and collided with a tree I don't have.
- The other car collided with mine without giving warning of its intention.
- I thought my window was down, but I found out it wasn't open when I put my head through it.
- I collided with a stationary truck coming the other way.
- A truck backed through my windshield into my wife's face.
- The guy was all over the road. I had to swerve a number of times before I hit him.
- I pulled away from the side of the road, glanced at my mother-in-law, and headed over the embankment.
- In an attempt to kill a fly, I drove into a telephone pole.
- I had been driving for forty years when I fell asleep at the wheel and had an accident.
- I was on my way to the doctor with rear end trouble when my universal joint gave way causing me to have an accident.
- As I approached the intersection a sign suddenly appeared in a place where no stop sign had ever appeared before. I was unable to stop in time to avoid the accident.
- To avoid hitting the bumper of the car in front of me I struck the pedestrian.
- My car was legally parked as it backed into the other vehicle.

- An invisible car came from out of nowhere, struck my car, and vanished.
- I told the police I was not injured, but on removing my hat found that I had a fractured skull.
- The pedestrian had no idea which direction to run so I ran him over.
- I saw a slow moving, sad faced old gentleman as he bounced off the roof of my car.
- I was thrown from my car as it left the road. I was later found in a ditch by some stray cows.

SAFETY EXPERTS SAY SCHOOL BUS PASSENGERS SHOULD BE BELTED

KNUCKLEHEAD IN THE SPOTLIGHT

MAYBE SHE SHOULD'VE CALLED A TOE TRUCK

If there's one thing Bonnie Booth has to be thankful about, it's that she didn't have a pimple on her forehead.

When the thirty-eight-year-old Muncie, Indiana, woman couldn't stand the discomfort of having a callus on her right foot, she decided to take matters into her own hands—by blowing off her big toe with a shotgun.

"It was just one of them simple medical procedures," Booth said from her bed at Muncie's Ball Hospital only a day after the makeshift operation. "The only difference is, I didn't have no doctor do it."

At first, Booth—a self-confessed "hillbilly"—was content to let her throbbing digit clear up on its own. But, according to Muncie Police Lt. Charles Hensley, she started worrying that the toe would become infected because it "hurt real bad."

"Well, what I done first, on Sunday, I took a razor blade and I cut a little of it to try to ease the pain. But then it didn't work. So Monday I decided to just go ahead and shoot it off," Booth said as casually as if she had switched to cotton swabs after failing to dig wax out of her ear with a finger. "I kinda figured *that* would take care of it, more or less."

At least no one could accuse her of acting irresponsibly. Before performing the "simple medical procedure," Booth was sure to administer what she called "proper anesthetics"—in the form of "two or three beers" and *a gallon of vodka*.

"I drank it straight from the jug," Booth said proudly before sneaking a long drag from her cigarette and blowing the smoke through an open hospital window. "That's the best way to drink it."

Although some may have trouble stomaching—both figuratively and literally—her claim that she consumed an entire gallon of straight 80-proof alcohol, Booth was apparently telling the truth: After escorting her to the hospital, police measured Booth's blood alcohol content at 0.42 percent.

"I don't drink that much every day," the divorced mother said. "Just when I wanna get drunk."

Following the gory amputation, the shoeless Booth hobbled to a neighbor's house and asked the resident to call 911. Then she found her way back into her living room, cracked open another brewski, and waited for an ambulance to arrive.

With the callus gone, Booth thought her troubles were finally over. But according to her live-in boyfriend—a stocky man who identified himself as "Skinner"—her problems were only just beginning.

About a week after Booth's release from the hospital, "they had this live-in nurse drop by," Skinner said, actually referring to a visiting nurse sent on a routine follow-up visit to the couple's home, "and I guess Bonnie went ahead and told her she was gonna kill herself. So the lady went and called the police."

But the alleged suicide threat was nothing but a misunderstanding, Booth said.

"I was feelin' a little low that day, you know?" she explained. "So this nurse come in and I says to her, 'I oughta just go and kill myself.' That's all. It's one of them things you say but you don't mean nothin' by it. Then, she packed up and left . . . and I thought that was it."

But unfortunately for Booth, that *wasn't* it. Less than an hour later she heard voices outside her house. She peered through the window and saw a group of police officers talking to Skinner, who had just returned from searching for the couple's lost dog.

After seizing Booth's .410-gauge shotgun, authorities once again brought her to the hospital—only this time she was admitted to the psychiatric ward.

"They locked me in the nuthouse for a whole week," a bitter Booth recalled. "Can you believe it? A whole week in the nuthouse, all on accounta me sayin' that to the nurse. I guess they realized I wasn't gonna kill myself, 'cause they let me out."

Even to this day, Booth can't understand why the shooting caused such a commotion.

"Welp, my callus was hurtin' my toe and I shot it off," Booth said matter-of-factly. "Now I ain't got no callus problem no more."

But she ain't got no big toe no more, either, right?

"Oh, I got four toes," Booth was quick to point out. "Plus a stub."

CHAPTER II

KNUCKLEHEADS IN COURT

A man arrested for possession of drugs in Michigan tried to have the charge dropped by telling the judge he was searched without a warrant.

The prosecutor, however, argued that a warrant wasn't needed because police saw a large bulge in the defendant's jacket, so they had good reason to suspect he was armed.

Claiming the arresting officer was lying, the man—who happened to be wearing the same jacket—handed the garment to the judge. The magistrate reached into the pocket in question and pulled out a huge bag of cocaine.

He laughed so hard, he called for a five-minute recess to compose himself.

When Jorge Rodriguez went before a municipal judge in Kenosha, Wisconsin, he had a conspicuous, smug look on his face.

The twenty-two-year-old man—charged with driving under the influence after he hit a parked car—pleaded guilty to the crime, but still expected to be sent home after the court proceedings. After the judge reprimanded him for his irresponsible behavior, Rodriguez reached into his pocket and pulled out his ace in the hole: a "get out of jail free" card, which had been distributed as a campaign gimmick during a recent election for sheriff.

Despite the accused man's ticket to freedom, the magistrate fined Rodriguez an undisclosed amount and sentenced him to probation.

"Clearly, the defendant had the impression it was legitimate," a prosecutor later told reporters.

═════════

COURTROOM QUOTE: From official records found in an anonymous courtroom somewhere in the United States . . .

Lawyer (to defendant): "Was that the same nose you broke as a child?"

═════════

Criminals sentenced to life in prison have been known to request the death penalty to avoid spending the rest of their lives behind bars. But an accused murderer in Tucson, Arizona, made the request *before* a verdict was reached—to prove his innocence.

Tucson police accused Robert Joe Moody of robbing and murdering two women in November 1993 to get money for his drug habit. But Moody—who acted as his own attorney during the three-week debacle—claimed he committed the deplorable crimes because . . . well, because outer space aliens told him to.

To top it off, Moody asked Superior Court Judge Howard Hantman to sentence him to death so the aliens could bring him back to life. Once that was accomplished, Moody argued, the court would see he was telling the truth.

Although a defense psychologist testified that Moody suffered from a multiple personality disorder, Hantman ruled the defendant was mentally competent at the time of the murders. He granted Moody's request, sentencing him to die for the slayings.

Moody, who received the news on his thirty-seventh birthday, addressed the court before his sentence was handed down. He said, "We have finally come to the point where I get my birthday wish. I hope you grant the appropriate sentence to allow me to complete my mission."

Courtroom observers said Moody was "thrilled" when Hantman made the announcement.

It's no wonder Moody lost his case; he was forced to stage his defense without his key witnesses. Before the trial, the judge scratched several people from Moody's witness list, including several UFO abductees, the late Senator Barry Goldwater, and former presidents Jimmy Carter and Gerald Ford.

═════════

COURTROOM QUOTE: You might think the judicial system could never be so wacky, but this Marx Brothers–like exchange actually happened in an American courtroom . . .

Lawyer: "I show you Exhibit three and ask you if you recognize that picture."

Witness: "That's me."

Lawyer: "Were you present when that picture was taken?"

═════════

COURTROOM QUOTE: Another gem spoken like a true attorney . . .

"Now, Doctor, isn't it true that when a person dies in his sleep, in most cases he just passes quietly away and doesn't know anything about it until the next morning?"

═════════

In Florida, attorneys entering Judge Leonard Fleet's courtroom are always sure to bring their documents, exhibits, notes, and *a bag of groceries*.

Fleet—who some might describe as "meticulous"—was sick of sluggish lawyers missing his imposed deadlines. So in November 1995, he wrote up a list of rules, warning if even one of the rules was violated, he'd punish the guilty party by forcing the unlucky sap to shop for diapers or food.

Before long, dozens of high-class attorneys were pushing squeaky shopping carts through the aisles of local grocery stores, buying such items as disposable diapers, mayonnaise, or Fleet's personal favorite, canned tuna. Fleet would then hand the goods over to a worthy charity.

By January—less than two months later—a whopping 360 lawyers had been penalized under the directive. Fleet made sure they got his point by ordering them to do all the shopping themselves and forbidding them from charging clients for time or expenses.

"In almost every case, the attorneys have done it with good humor," Fleet told reporters. "They even tease me about it: 'If you go before Judge Fleet, be sure to bring tuna fish.' "

———

COURTROOM QUOTE: A masterful display of professional grilling . . .

Lawyer: "Do you know how far pregnant you are now?"

Defendant: "I'll be three months on November eighth."

Lawyer: "Apparently, then, the date of conception was August eighth?"

Defendant: "Yes."

Lawyer: "What were you doing at that time?"

Lewis Elwood Jordan was hating life.

As if being accused of murder wasn't bad enough, Jordan found his new barred sleeping quarters to be less than satisfactory, and he wasn't getting along with his lawyer.

Despite the tension between the men, defending attorney Jake Waldrop presented Jordan's case in Atlanta Federal Court. Apparently dissatisfied with Waldrop's argument, Jordan—who was only half dressed to protest the jail's living environment—whipped out his little cellmate and urinated on Waldrop's leg.

After the resulting courtroom fracas had died down, Judge Robert Vining, Jr., ordered Waldrop to continue outlining his client's defense.

"I have made my point, Judge, in writing," Waldrop responded. "I guess Mr. Jordan has made *his* point, not verbally, [but] by urinating on my leg."

———

It's a good thing baseball jerseys display only the *last* names of players. Because if first names were included, a five-year-old boy in Stockholm, Sweden, would've encountered significant problems in Little League had his parents won their court case.

Standing before a judge in a Stockholm appeals court, the unidentified couple fought to overturn a decision that denied their request to saddle their son with a forty-three-letter name.

The proposed name: "Brfxxccxxmnpccccllllmmnprxvclmnck-ssqlbblllll6." Its pronunciation: "Albin."

The parents argued the name was a "pregnant, expressionistic development that we see as an artistic creation."

The judge rejected the appeal in record time.

═══════════

COURTROOM QUOTES: If you're considering a career in the legal profession, don't let an inability to grasp the obvious hold you back. It didn't stop the following trial attorneys . . .

Lawyer: "Mrs. Jones, do you believe you are emotionally stable?"
Mrs. Jones: "I used to be."
Lawyer: "How many times have you committed suicide?"

Defendant: "He told me, he says, 'I have to kill you because you can identify me.'"
Lawyer: "Did he kill you?"

Lawyer: "She had three children, right?"
Witness: "Yes."
Lawyer: "How many were boys?"
Witness: "None."
Lawyer: "Were there girls?"

* * *

Lawyer: "You say that the stairs went down to the basement?"
Defendant: "Yes."
Lawyer: "And these stairs, did they go up also?"

———

It was a speech that would've made Perry Mason proud.

In an attempt to have his client's bail lowered, a Pennsylvania attorney delivered one the most eloquent dissertations of his career. After outlining a plethora of reasons why the defendant— who had been arrested on drug charges—wasn't likely to flee, the legal eagle took a moment to bask in the euphoria of a job well done.

His inner haughtiness lasted only a moment, however, as he was wrenched back to reality by a hubbub that arose in the courtroom. While the lawyer was busy telling the judge how trustworthy his client was, the defendant had somehow slipped through an open window and made his way onto the building's roof.

The lawyer quietly packed up his briefcase while his client led frazzled police officers on a rooftop chase.

———

Drug users do the wackiest things.

In December 1995 police in Nashua, New Hampshire, arrested James Mascetta and charged him with dispensing illegal narcotics—in a *courtroom*.

The unexpected drug bust occurred after a bailiff saw the forty-year-old Mascetta allegedly hand a packet of heroin to a woman sitting at the defendant's table. The woman was in court to face arraignment on her *own* drug charges.

———————

At the age of seventy-three you'd think the side effects of Mary Verdev's accidental blow to the head would almost be *welcome*.

But when the Wisconsin woman began experiencing "spontaneous orgasms" after a 300-pound bingo board came crashing down on her head, she brought the case to a Milwaukee circuit court.

The incident occurred in 1990 when Verdev was feverishly involved in an intense game of bingo at St. Florian Catholic Church in Milwaukee. As she searched her card for the number that had just been announced, the giant electronic board—which the church used to display numbers that had already been called—broke free of its restraints and plummeted from the stage. Unfortunately, Verdev's skull was right in its line of descent.

Bringing the case before Judge Patrick J. Madden, Verdev claimed not only did she start experiencing uncontrollable orgasms—sometimes in "clusters"—she also suffered almost $90,000 in physical injuries and suddenly found herself sexually attracted to other women.

James Green, an attorney for the church, claimed Verdev was "dishonest," saying she suffered nothing more than a small lump on her head and a modest bruise on her arm.

Furthermore, he said, "It is unexplained in modern medicine how a bump on the head can alter sexual orientation or cause recurring orgasms."

Judge Madden, apparently seeing some sense in Green's argument, ordered Verdev to undergo a psychological exam. Verdev never complied.

After it floundered about in the system for six years, the case was finally thrown out of court.

═══════

While the United States justice system promises "fair and speedy" resolutions to cases brought before a judge, many legal virtuosos argue both aspects of the pledge aren't necessarily pursued by the courts. Instead, *defendants* are more interested in fair trials while *prosecutors* do their best to keep the proceedings speedy.

Naturally, there are always exceptions.

Take Valdamair Morelos. When the thirty-five-year-old man was tried for murder in 1994, he threw all notions of fairness to the wind, doing his damnedest to hurry things along.

At a pretrial hearing in San Jose, California, Morelos willingly confessed, asking the judge to sentence him to death. To his consternation, however, California law requires a trial in a court of law in all capital cases, so he was forced to be inconvenienced by an official legal hearing. To make matters worse, his case wasn't scheduled to see the inside of a courtroom until January 1995— *the following year*.

So, when his trial finally began, Morelos did his best to expedite the operation by *helping the prosecution*. For example, after the prosecuting attorney described the murder to the judge, Morelos shouted out, "I blindfolded him, too!"

———

COURTROOM QUOTES: One of the keys to being a good trial lawyer is to know which questions to ask. Here are some more humdingers from America's courtrooms:

- "The youngest son, the twenty-year-old, how old is he?"
- "Were you alone or by yourself?"
- "Do you have any children or anything of that kind?"

———

While the appeals system was set up to help convicted criminals who feel they were deprived of a fair trial the first time around, you'd probably have no trouble finding repeat defendants who'd tell you the whole thing is a crock.

Take the Arizona man who was convicted of drug possession in 1995. Although he was convinced his trial was nothing more than a judicial lampoon, his appeal was rejected by the U.S. Supreme Court in January 1996.

His reason for the appeal: There were no fat people on the jury.

———

In the legal system's defense, the U.S. Court of Appeals doesn't leave *everyone* out in the cold. In March 1996, a New York court gave the go-ahead to order a new trial for a man serving the tenth year of his eighteen-year drug-related sentence.

Inmate Dale Tippins contended he was worthy of a new trial because his lawyer had napped through his first shot at justice. After hearing testimony from two jurors—one saying he heard the lawyer snoring on numerous occasions, the other recalling he slept through "sixty-five percent" of a key witness's testimony —the court had no realistic alternative to granting the request.

When handing down the decision, however, the judge included what some might perceive as a veiled "don't press your luck" addendum. He noted, "There are states of drowsiness that come over everyone from time to time during [a trial]."

———

An unconfirmed tale from the "likely story" department, as told by an anonymous court reporter in Arizona:

A woman asked a judge to grant her a divorce from her philandering husband, claiming he'd committed adultery on numerous occasions. To add insult to injury, the dirty dog broke his wedding vows *right in the couple's bedroom*—the forlorn plaintiff testified she occasionally returned home in the middle of the night and heard her husband and a strange woman making "grunting noises" in the bedroom.

While the husband confessed to sharing time with a woman in the bedroom, he offered a perfectly reasonable explanation for the seemingly incriminating deed: Having recently set up a new pool table in the bedroom, he yearned for the challenge of racking up against a worthy opponent. As things turned out, the only adversary he could find was the woman in question. As for the "grunting noises," he innocently explained his wife had eavesdropped on "sounds of excitement when we made tough shots."

The judge granted the divorce, rationalizing, "All the shots would be tough when you're playing in a dark room in the middle of the night."

In Stanton, Michigan, a man found guilty of assaulting his wife was let off with nothing more than a slap on the wrist. Literally.

In January 1996, Judge Joel Gehrke found Stewart Marshall guilty of pushing his wife to the floor during an argument. After announcing his verdict, Gehrke summoned Marshall to the bench and asked him to hold out his hand. Then Gehrke gave him a light slap on the wrist, telling the defendant, "Don't do that!"

Understandably, do-gooders all over the country were appalled at Gehrke's seemingly mild sentence. Gehrke, on the other hand, thought the punishment was justified because the wife allegedly slept with Marshall's brother and gave birth to Marshall's nephew.

Courtroom quote: Another unscripted legal laugh . . .

Lawyer: "Do you recall approximately the time that you examined the body of Mr. Edington?"

Coroner: "It was in the evening. The autopsy started about eight-thirty P.M."

Lawyer: "And Mr. Edington was dead at the time, is that correct?"

Coroner: "No, you stupid, he was sitting on the table wondering why I was doing an autopsy!"

KNUCKLEHEAD IN
THE SPOTLIGHT

FUN & GAMES
WITH TINY TIM

What's Tiny Tim been up to since he tiptoed through the tulips back in 1968?

At last sighting, he was careening through an airport. On an out-of-control electric cart, no less.

On June 28, 1996, the ukulele-strumming *singer*—to use the term loosely—landed at Philadelphia International Airport for an appearance later that evening. Apparently having some time to kill—but not wanting to waste any valuable energy while killing it—the seventy-three-year-old Tiny used his "star" status to commandeer one of the airport's electric carts.

That's when all hell broke loose.

Within moments Tiny—whose real name is Herbert Khaury—was seen frantically trying to steer the speeding cart as it barreled through a cluster of suitcases and continued toward the ticket counter.

Esther Arthur, en route to her son's wedding, was one of several passengers waiting to check in.

"I was standing in line waiting to get our tickets validated," the sixty-seven-year-old grandmother said. "Then all of a sudden somehow from somewhere this cart came from someplace. I don't even know where it came from. The next thing I knew, I was knocked out."

According to witnesses, Tiny's cart ran out of control for at least fifty feet before injuring Arthur and another passenger. But Arthur, a resident of Lawnside, New Jersey, said she didn't even see it coming.

"I was standing there and he came right through the crowd," Arthur said. "I said, 'Oh, God!' I didn't even know what had happened. You know, one minute you're standing there and the next minute you're lying on the floor and this thing's running over the top of you while you're wonderin' what in the world is going on."

After making short work of the helpless woman, Tiny continued his onslaught and slammed into an unidentified man, pinning him up against a wall.

Now, here's where things get a little sketchy: When Philadelphia's finest finally showed up, Tiny fingered *another* man as the driver. While he admitted tossing down two beers just prior to the melee, he told police he was merely a passenger in the uncontrollable cart. His apparent fall guy corroborated the story.

Neither Arthur nor the other victim could positively identify the driver, so the befuddled cops sent Tiny Tim on his way—to perform at a minor league baseball doubleheader in Reading.

"I was flipped over and knocked down on the floor and then it ran over my feet and legs," Arthur lamented from her bed in Woodside. "My legs started hurtin' me so bad I couldn't even move. I had to just lay there. I didn't know what he did or said because I don't even know what happened."

Arthur was taken to a local hospital, where she was treated for a broken pelvic bone and two fractures in her foot. The other traveler's injuries were not disclosed, but Arthur said "he got a neck and back injury, I think it was."

But the story doesn't end there. The following day, after hearing of the crooner's "innocent" plea, a handful of witnesses stepped forward to debunk his recollection of the crash. The case was reopened and, as of press time, is still being investigated.

While Arthur doesn't remember much about what transpired immediately after the crash, her granddaughter—who was traveling with her—saw the former pop icon when he strolled past them a few minutes earlier.

"After he went by she said, 'There goes Tiny Tim,' but I didn't see him," Arthur recalled. "I didn't know he was gonna go get a cart and come back and knock me down."

KNUCKLEHEADS IN CRIME

After months of planning, a small-time criminal in Columbia, Tennessee, decided to pull off the ultimate crime: bank robbery.

So on March 28, 1995, the man grabbed a gun, ran through the front door of the bank, and yelled, "Give me your money!" But instead of screams, the bandit's bold entrance solicited *snickers* from the people in the building. Confused, the man lowered his pistol and looked around. It was then that he realized he wasn't in a bank; it had closed down almost seven months before and was now the home of an insurance company.

"I didn't think he was serious at first," one of the insurance agents told police, "so I laughed."

The would-be bank robber then turned to the employee and asked, "This ain't a bank anymore?" When the employee shook his head, the disappointed holdup man started to leave. Then, apparently having second thoughts, he turned around and ordered the employees to empty their wallets and purses.

He made off with $127.

———

In January 1995, Ohio police arrested a teenager and charged him with breaking into a local florist, where he made off with seven hanging plants.

Detectives tracked down the suspect by following a trail of petals to his nearby home.

———

In January 1996, a blizzard dumped more than fourteen inches of snow on parts of the northern East Coast. The aftermath—which resulted in miles of roads being shut down—produced stories that will be told for years to come. But few are as unusual as the story of eighty-year-old William Wolfe.

Suffering from a kidney infection, Wolfe decided to brave the storm and walk a mile to a medical office. As he approached the door, a woman walked up and started a conversation with the Paterson, New Jersey, resident. After learning of his ailment, the woman said she knew of a doctor who'd give him a shot for only fifteen dollars. Since the doctor lived right around the corner, Wolfe agreed to follow the woman to the doctor's home.

The woman—who was later identified as thirty-one-year-old Gertrude Williams, a convicted prostitute—led Wolfe down an alley, coming to a stop at the rear entrance of a private home. Wolfe became uneasy and told Williams he had changed his mind.

Outraged, Williams demanded the fifteen dollars anyway. When Wolfe refused, she punched him in the mouth, knocking his false teeth to the snow-covered ground. She then scooped up the man's uppers and ran away.

After Wolfe reported the incident, Paterson police launched an investigation, which eventually led them to Williams.

"She took us to a crack house on Auburn Street, reached into a coat pocket in a closet, and pulled them out," Detective Timothy Jordan told reporters. "They were still in good shape, too."

Two weeks after the dentures were stolen, police returned them to their rightful owner.

"I was lucky to get them back," Wolfe said. "I've been eating a lot of soft food."

———

Miami police charged three teenagers with robbing a local grocery store after the inept felons ending up *shooting each other*.

The incident occurred on February 27, 1996, when Jeanis Caty, eighteen, Wesley Steny, sixteen, and an unidentified accomplice strolled into the supermarket brandishing guns. Pointing their weapons at the surprised checkout clerks, the youths ordered them to open the cash register drawers and hit the floor.

Now, here's where their problems began: Instead of walking around the counter, the nervous Caty decided to lean *across* the checkout stand to retrieve the money from the drawer. In doing so, he accidentally fired his gun, striking Steny in the thigh.

Reeling from the pain, Steny fell to the ground, inadvertently squeezing the trigger on his own handgun in the process. The shot somehow managed to pierce *both* of Caty's hands and his leg.

While the third suspect did all he could to maintain his composure, the injured teens grabbed about $200 from the cash registers. Then they limped out the door, leaving a trail of blood behind them.

According to Detective Tom Pellechio of Miami's Metro-Dade Police Department, the culprits weren't hard to track down: Police simply drove to the nearest hospital, where they found the injured holdup men sitting in the emergency room.

"I've had robbers shoot themselves before, but I never had two robbers shoot each other," Pellechio said.

———

In New Canaan, Connecticut, someone removed the tires from a car parked at a train station, stole the brakes, and put the tires back on.

———

No one would accuse them of being landscaping aficionados, but Jess and Judy Daniel of Grapevine, Texas, *liked* the little plastic duck they proudly displayed in their front yard. One morning, Jess walked outside to catch the bus for work, and the duck was gone. Since the synthetic fowl was valued at less than twenty dollars, the Daniels didn't bother calling police. In fact, they pretty much forgot about the pilfered duck—until a year later.

Almost twelve months to the day of the theft, Judy walked outside to get the morning paper—and there was the duck, in the exact same spot it had been taken from. Sitting next to the lawn ornament was a photo album with the words "The World Quack Tour 95" neatly printed on the cover.

Opening the picture book, the Daniels found forty-three vacation photos, each taken at a different place. There was a picture of the duck watching a gaggle of geese at Hyde Park in London; a snapshot of it taking in the sights at Notre Dame in Paris; and even a photo of the duck looking up at the Gateway Arch in St. Louis.

The Daniels say they have no idea who stole the duck, why they took it on vacation, or why they returned it.

In Roanoke, Virginia, a woman was arrested for stealing more than five hundred pieces of mail from her neighbors' mailboxes. A judge found the woman to be sane—but stated that the defendant had an "irresistible impulse" to steal other people's mail.

The judge sentenced the woman to house arrest, allowing her full freedom only on Sundays, when there is no mail delivery.

MAN SHOOTS NEIGHBOR WITH MACHETE

In a report filed with a local police department in Tennessee, a couple reported their driveway missing. According to their statement, thieves had removed all the gravel and plowed the ground beneath it.

———

A fifty-five-year-old Brooklyn, New York, man was arrested and charged with possession of counterfeit property after he was caught returning *non*returnable bottles to a New Hyde Park grocery store.

According to police records, the man collected bar codes from soda bottles and made photocopies of them before taping the counterfeit codes to nonrefundable bottles. Then he used a bottle redeeming machine at a local Edward's supermarket to collect the five-cent refund on each of the containers.

When arresting the man at the scene, police found over a thousand bar codes and bags of bottles in his possession.

———

For most people, a good meal is important before heading off to work.

But for a would-be robber in Fire Island, New York, a Mexican dinner proved to be his undoing.

On October 30, 1994, the residents of a Fire Island home were stirred from their sleep by "strange sounds" coming from their living room. The husband got up to search the house but found nothing.

Unable to fall back asleep right away, the husband and wife were talking when they heard more strange noises. Only this time the disturbance strangely resembled someone with a gas problem.

Searching the house again, the man followed the sounds to a closet, where he detected an "unpleasant odor." He opened the door to find fifty-six-year-old Richard Magpiong squatting between the clothes.

He quickly closed and locked the door, holding Magpiong hostage until police arrived.

While most professionals choose the summer months for their vacations, a would-be burglar in Williamsport, Pennsylvania, found out he should've taken the winter off—the hard way.

On February 2, 1996, Henry Carlton apparently decided to break into the office of a Williamsport real estate firm. So, warmly bundled in two sweatshirts and a bulky winter coat, the forty-one-year-old found an unlocked basement window and attempted to lower himself through it.

Under normal circumstances the average-sized Carlton might've succeeded in fitting through the 15-by-18-inch window, but the extra layers of clothing proved to be too much for the modest entryway. Halfway through the window, Carlton found himself firmly lodged between the wooden frame—his legs dangling inside the building, his head and upper torso outside.

Although Carlton's family reported him missing later that night, it wasn't until four days later that an employee of the office found the unlucky felon—still wedged in the window, frozen to death.

"This is one of those rare situations where dressing warmly was the *wrong* thing to do," the employee said.

———

Most New York Police Department officers have come across their fair share of knuckleheads. One seventeen-year veteran (who has asked for anonymity) told us one of his favorite stories.

In the late 1980s a recently married Manhattan couple had just finished taking in a Broadway show. Unable to find a vacant cab on bustling Broadway, they decided to cut down a dimly lit side street in hopes of locating an available taxi on the next main thoroughfare, which usually had less traffic at that hour of the night.

After walking about two hundred yards the pair was approached by a gun-wielding man, who the officer described as "weighing in excess of three hundred pounds." The obese mugger told the newlyweds to hand over their cash or he'd shoot both of them. Reluctantly, the woman handed the man her purse while her husband reached into his back pocket for his wallet.

The gunman—apparently thinking the man was about to pull out a weapon—jumped toward his surprised victims. In doing so, he tripped, fell to the ground, and dropped his firearm. The quick-thinking husband kicked the gun into the gutter, and the couple ran back to the theater, where they called police.

When officers arrived about fifteen minutes later, they found the hefty thief—still lying on the ground, struggling to get up onto his feet.

———————

A twenty-two-year-old burglar was arrested on January 19, 1996, after he was caught sleeping on the job.

The man, who worked as a locksmith in Kuala Lumpur, Malaysia, had just gone on a crime spree that included burglarizing several offices and breaking into a safe. Apparently, the night of looting must've taken something out of him, because after cleaning out his last office, he decided to take a nap on the floor.

A worker found the thief snoring away when he opened the office at eight A.M. the following day. He was still asleep when police arrived.

———————

ARSON SUSPECT IS HELD IN MASSACHUSETTS FIRE

An unidentified man walked into a bank in Manhattan, placed a brown paper bag on the counter, and told the teller there was a bomb inside. He said he'd blow the place to smithereens if she didn't hand over a stack of twenty-dollar bills.

After collecting $380 from the frightened employee, the man ran from the bank, leaving the bag sitting on the counter. The manager called the police, who sent out dozens of bomb squad officers. After putting on their gear and evacuating the entire bank and the two bottom floors of the buildings around it, they finally opened the bag.

It contained a pair of dirty pants.

———————

A shoplifting suspect in St. George, Utah, was arrested after his escape attempt was thwarted by a pole.

Twenty-one-year-old Steven Kemble was shopping at Tom Tom CDs & Tapes when he allegedly decided to swipe a compact disc from the store's shelf. An alert clerk witnessed the theft, however, and detained Kemble while another employee called police.

While they were waiting for officers to arrive, Kemble decided to make a break for it. After running through the main entrance, Kemble ran smack into a pillar in front of the store, knocking himself unconscious.

———————

When police in Melbourne, Australia, finally catch up with a group of wanted men, the felons will undoubtedly take their punishment at full attention.

Not that it'll have anything to do with bravery or honor. You might say, however, it'll have something to do with *hard time*.

In June 1996 burglars broke into a Melbourne clinic and filched several dozen bottles of medication to treat impotence. Many of the bottles contained a drug that causes five-day erections.

A police spokesman said the drugs weren't fatal, but "they can cause extreme discomfort."

"We are looking for someone who is very embarrassed or very tired," the spokesman said.

A Bangladesh man became the talk of Kuwait when he claimed he was kidnapped, beaten, and raped by three women.

On June 12, 1996, the unidentified sanitation worker had made his daily pilgrimage from Bangladesh to Kuwait when he was attacked by three thirtysomething-year-old women. They forced their victim into a car and drove him to a secluded area in the desert, where one of the women asked if he'd have sex with her.

Undoubtedly thinking of his wife in Bangladesh, the man naturally responded, "No."

This threw the pack of sex-crazed kidnappers into a rage. Refusing to take no for an answer, the nymphomaniacs tore off every stitch of the man's clothing and beat the living daylights out of him. Then one of the women bullied him into having sex with her.

Once the sexual predator's needs were met, she and her cohorts unwound by beating up their weak-kneed victim a second time. Then, doing the courteous thing, they drove him back to town and dropped him off at work.

As quoted by a reporter for Kuwait's *al-Watan* newspaper, the man stressed the fact that his attacker "forced him to commit adultery with her."

AN EAR TO REMEMBER

If you happen to see Chicago resident Mark Webb holding a telephone receiver up to his stomach, rest assured he's *not crazy*—he's probably just trying to hear the caller.

In late April 1995, Webb—a night-shift supervisor at Cosmopolitan Textile Rental Service—fired one of his employees after the man allegedly refused to turn down his radio. Outraged, the worker grabbed Webb's head and *bit off his ear*.

"I was getting some complaints from neighbors across the alley about the radio being played too loud," Webb recalled from his bed at the University of Chicago Medical Center. After asking the rockin' employee to lower the volume, Webb said the man "cursed me out and went to lunch. When he came back, I called him to my office and asked him what he really wanted to say . . . and he cursed me out again. So I told him to punch out and give me his key."

The agitated truck unloader—who Webb said tipped the scales at approximately three hundred pounds—stormed out of the office as Webb began filling out his discharge forms. A short while later the man came back.

"I was just finishing up the paperwork and I heard some footsteps coming toward me," the 168-pound Webb said. "By the time

I looked up, he was coming down on my head."

Pulling Webb's noggin toward him, the employee wrapped his lips around his manager's right ear and bit down hard—completely severing the auricle from Webb's head.

"I felt pain on my ear, but I had no idea he had bit the ear off," Webb said. "Then I saw it fall out of his mouth, and I knew."

The employee was arrested and Webb was rushed to the hospital, where surgeons promptly reattached the severed ear to his body. Or, to be more precise, *his stomach*.

According to doctors, the ear had lost most of its blood, and they hoped the capillary-rich region of the abdomen would replenish the tissue.

"They stuck it right above my pubic area," Webb explained, raising his hospital gown to display his bandaged torso. "It's a little bit uncomfortable."

After two failed attempts to reattach the chewed-off ear, doctors were forced to abandon their efforts. Still, Webb seemed to take the unfortunate incident in stride.

"If I would've known he was hungry, I would've bought him a sandwich," he said.

CHAPTER IV

KNUCKLE-HEADLINES

To outsiders, the life of a newspaper reporter might seem glamorous. But any well-respected journalist will be the first to disagree.

A real estate agent only has to know about real estate. A cop only has to know law and order. Jimmy Dean only has to know sausage. But to do his job, a newspaper reporter has to know more about real estate than Donald Trump, more about law and order than J. Edgar Hoover, and more about Jimmy Dean's sausage than his own wife.

And, just to make things interesting, the newsman's path to the truth is littered with spokespersons, spin doctors, press agents, PR geeks, and other professional liars who work night and day punching up the facts and hiding the truth. Nonetheless, the facts have to be sorted, sifted, sniffed, and squeezed until the truth finally comes dripping out. Once the facts have produced the truth, reporters have to present it in the vocabulary of a six-year-old in the amount of time it takes the average slack-jawed American to have a bowel movement.

Yet, ironically, after all of the blood, sweat, and tears are invested in a story, the reporter has nothing to do with what many view as the most important part: the headline.

Weary editors, forced to toil over a computer terminal each day searching for errors in miles of boring copy, are saddled with the responsibility of writing an eye-catching, informative, colorful headline for each story they edit. To make their jobs even *more* difficult, the snappy titles have to fit in a predetermined space left by the layout crew.

It's only natural that these pressures—compounded by constant deadlines—are bound to result in mistakes. Following is a list of headlines taken from the pages of newspapers from all over the country. Look for others throughout the book, too.

═══════════

Iraqi Head Seeks Arms

Prostitutes Appeal to Pope

Panda Mating Fails; Veterinarian Takes Over

Lung Cancer in Women Mushrooms

TEACHER STRIKES IDLE KIDS

SHOT OFF WOMAN'S LEG HELPS NICKLAUS TO 66

PLANE TOO CLOSE TO GROUND, CRASH PROBE TOLD

MINERS REFUSE TO WORK AFTER DEATH

STOLEN PAINTING FOUND BY THREE

TWO SOVIET SHIPS COLLIDE, ONE DIES

2 SISTERS REUNITED AFTER 18 YEARS AT CHECKOUT COUNTER

NEVER WITHHOLD HERPES INFECTION FROM LOVED ONE

DRUNKEN DRIVERS PAID $1,000 IN '84

WAR DIMS HOPE FOR PEACE

IF STRIKE ISN'T SETTLED QUICKLY, IT MAY LAST AWHILE

COLD WAVE LINKED TO TEMPERATURES

MAN IS FATALLY SLAIN

ENFIELD COUPLE SLAIN; POLICE SUSPECT HOMICIDE

MILK DRINKERS ARE TURNING TO POWDER

FARMER BILL DIES IN HOUSE

HOUSE PASSES GAS TAX ONTO SENATE

TWO CONVICTS EVADE NOOSE, JURY HUNG

QUEEN MARY HAVING BOTTOM SCRAPED

IS THERE A RING OF DEBRIS AROUND URANUS?

CHILD'S STOOL GREAT FOR USE IN GARDEN

ORGAN FESTIVAL ENDS IN SMASHING CLIMAX

AUTOS KILLING 110 A DAY, LET'S RESOLVE TO DO BETTER

SMOKERS ARE PRODUCTIVE, BUT DEATH CUTS EFFICIENCY

BLIND WOMAN GETS NEW KIDNEY FROM DAD SHE HASN'T SEEN IN YEARS

SOMETHING WENT WRONG IN JET CRASH, EXPERTS SAY

DEATH CAUSES LONELINESS, FEELING OF ISOLATION

REAGAN WINS ON BUDGET, BUT MORE LIES AHEAD

STUDY FINDS SEX, PREGNANCY LINK

ALCOHOL ADS PROMOTE DRINKING

MALLS TRY TO ATTRACT SHOPPERS

TOMATOES COME IN BIG, LITTLE, MEDIUM SIZES

DIRTY-AIR CITIES FAR DEADLIER THAN CLEAN ONES, STUDY SHOWS

FREE ADVICE: BUNDLE UP WHEN OUT IN THE COLD

BIBLE CHURCH'S FOCUS IS THE BIBLE

BITING NAILS CAN BE SIGN OF TENSENESS IN A PERSON

LACK OF BRAINS HINDERS RESEARCH

HOW WE FEEL ABOUT OURSELVES IS THE CORE OF SELF-ESTEEM,
    SAYS AUTHOR

FISH LURK IN STREAMS

RED TAPE HOLDS UP NEW BRIDGE

TYPHOON RIPS THROUGH CEMETERY; HUNDREDS DEAD

MAN STRUCK BY LIGHTNING FACES BATTERY CHARGE

NEW STUDY OF OBESITY LOOKS FOR LARGER TEST GROUP

KIDS MAKE NUTRITIOUS SNACKS

CHEF THROWS HIS HEART INTO HELPING FEED NEEDY

LOCAL HIGH SCHOOL DROPOUTS CUT IN HALF

DEAF COLLEGE OPENS DOORS TO HEARING

OLD SCHOOL PILLARS ARE REPLACED BY ALUMNI

BANK DRIVE-IN WINDOW BLOCKED BY BOARD

FERTILE WOMAN DIES IN CLIMAX

(In Minnesota, there are towns called Fertile and Climax. The story that carried the headline was about a woman from Fertile who died in a car accident in Climax.)

CHAPTER V

KNUCKLEHEADS IN SUITS

A Laguna Beach man filed a lawsuit against his ex-wife, claiming she made him sign their divorce decree under "unreasonable pressure."

In a preliminary hearing, the unidentified man told the judge his wife hired two men to hold a burning flare up to his crotch while his estranged wife looked on. She then handed him a pen and told him to sign the papers "or else."

The suit also cited "psychological damages," claiming the man now breaks out in a cold sweat every time he has to sign his name.

Thirty-two-year-old Bob Glaser filed a $5.4 million lawsuit against the city of San Diego for "emotional trauma" he suffered at an Elton John–Billy Joel concert. Apparently, the lines for the women's rest room were too long, so a few of the female patrons decided to conduct their business in the men's room. Glaser's suit cited "emotional trauma," saying he became "extremely upset" when he saw a woman using a urinal.

———

In Chesapeake, Virginia, Robert Lee Brock—an inmate at the Chesapeake Correctional Facility—filed a $5 million lawsuit against *himself*.

In the suit, Brock accused himself of violating his religious beliefs and civil rights by getting himself drunk enough to commit a series of crimes. He wrote, "I want to pay myself five million dollars for my breach of rights, but ask the state to pay it in my behalf since I can't work and am a ward of the state."

The action was thrown out of court.

———

The Toronto-Dominion Bank in Toronto, Canada, filed a $3.5 million lawsuit against Edward Del Grande, claiming he didn't pay back a loan he had taken out to start a small business.

In turn, Del Grande countersued for $30 million, saying the bank should've known not to lend him so much money.

In Roanoke, Virginia, Janet S. Robinson filed a lawsuit seeking $100,000 in damages for an ankle injury she suffered when she was hit by a truck.

The action was brought against Kay-Bee Toys at Valley View Mall. The truck was a remote-controlled toy that was being operated by another customer in the store.

Robinson felt she deserved the money because of the "pain, humiliation, aggravation, and disability" she'd suffered.

———

In 1995, Etta Stephens of Tampa, Florida, filed a lawsuit against Barnett Bank, claiming the institution gave her a heart attack.

The incident occurred when Stephens received her money-market statement in the mail. Although the account should've contained around $20,000, the balance showed a grand total of "ZERO." Upon seeing this, Stephens clutched her bosom and fell to the ground.

Barnett officials apologized for the misunderstanding, blaming the erroneous balance on a "printing error."

———

In July 1995 a prisoner at a Pennsylvania state correctional facility filed a lawsuit against "Satan and his staff."

Inmate Gerald Mayo filed the suit in U.S. District Court, Pittsburgh, claiming the devil and his servants deliberately placed "obstacles" in his way, which caused his downfall and subsequent incarceration. In doing so, Mayo maintained, Satan had violated his constitutional rights.

In Mayo's eyes the action seemed like an open-and-shut case, but Judge Gerald Weber disagreed. Even if the allegations were true, Weber argued, he could do nothing to support the suit because Mayo couldn't prove that Satan lived within the boundaries of the court's jurisdiction. Besides, in order to file a lawsuit against someone, the plaintiff is responsible for providing the defendant's address so the legal papers could be delivered.

Weber threw the case out of court.

It's the number-one gripe among television weather forecasters: the grief they get from viewers when their predictions don't quite match the actual weather.

In Haifa, Israel, a woman took her grievance to the extreme. After a local meteorologist predicted sunshine, the woman left her house dressed for warm weather. Unfortunately, the shining sun missed its scheduled appearance—it rained all day.

Feeling betrayed and disgruntled, the woman filed a thousand-dollar claim against the television station and its weatherman, claiming her inappropriate attire caused her to catch the flu, miss four days' work, and run up $38 in medical expenses.

In addition to the financial compensation, the suit demanded a public apology from the weatherman.

In September 1995 a Texas man filed a lawsuit against a local television station and three of its anchors, claiming the on-camera personnel had been bombarding his mind with secret messages of "perverted lust and distracting TV illusions." The man also said the anchors would often "scream" and "breathe loud" at him. The suit claimed the harassment caused the loss of his facial hair, as well as hair "in the back."

When actress Julie Andrews was the only member of *Victor/Victoria* to be nominated for a Tony Award in 1995, she shocked Broadway by refusing the honor. But it wasn't the first time the nomination process had been questioned by a celebrity.

In 1994, comedian Jackie Mason told reporters he'd filed a $25 million lawsuit against the awards committee for failing to nominate him for *Jackie Mason: Politically Incorrect.*

Mason claimed the oversight was "an abridgment of my rights as a human being."

CHICK ACCUSES SOME OF HER MALE COLLEAGUES OF SEXISM

(referring to Los Angeles councilwoman Laura Chick)

CHAPTER VI

KNUCKLEHEADS IN PRISON

When Philadelphia's Walnut Street Jail opened in 1790, a whole new precedent was set for courts and prisons all over the country. Instead of using detention facilities to temporarily house convicted criminals while a harsher sentence was determined, the U.S. legal system began viewing long-term prison sentences as viable means of punishment. The theory—which is still accepted today—was that an appropriate duration of penitence, honest labor, and rehabilitation would convert deceitful criminals into honest, law-abiding citizens.

Maybe someone should let the prisoners know.

Every year, thousands of convicts file lawsuits against their respective states to protest what they see as less-than-satisfactory living conditions. In fact, between 1985 and 1995, no less than 15,848 actions were filed against New York *alone*.

According to New York City Councilman Tom Ognibene, taxpayers in the Empire State cough up more than $4 million a year to help bring jailbirds' "frivolous" cases to court.

Some examples from the nation's prison population:

- In New York, one inmate sued over the right to use pink towels instead of the prison-issued white ones.
- After a three-month stay at the South Bay Detention Center in San Diego, California, Richard Loritz filed a $2,000 suit against his jailers for refusing to let him use dental floss. Claiming the restriction netted him four cavities, Loritz said, "Despite several requests, the sheriff's deputies did not provide me with dental floss, which is a medical necessity."
- A New York prisoner charged the state with violating his civil rights by refusing to let him attend chapel services in the nude.
- Although Pennsylvania prison officials arranged for more than 150 medical examinations, Rocco Mancini—a resident of Huntingdon State Prison—accused them of failing to provide reasonable medical aid for a pain he suffered in his back and kidneys. Although he produced two exhibits at his hearing, the judge dismissed the case when it was discovered that the small pebbles were *not* kidney stones, as Mancini had claimed.
- Dissatisfied with the lunch hall's limited selection, one New York prisoner sued over his "constitutional right" to a salad with lunch.

- In 1985, Abdur-Rauf Muhammad charged Huntingdon State Prison officials with violating his "First Amendment right to practice religion" after he was reprimanded for disturbing other inmates. The other prisoners complained they couldn't sleep because Muhammad insisted on reciting Muslim chants at four A.M.
- One inmate at an unidentified jail sued the state for $1 million, claiming guards wouldn't refrigerate his ice cream sandwich so he could eat it later.
- Rendrick Sumlin filed a $3 million suit against Berks County Prison in Pennsylvania, alleging he didn't get adequate medical treatment after he was stung by a bee. He suffered no adverse reactions from the sting.
- Warren Barrage charged Huntingdon State Prison officials with "cruel and unusual punishment" after they deducted $104 from his inmate account. The suit was dismissed because the money had been taken to replace a mattress Barrage had destroyed.

***

A convicted mugger's well-planned escape from a Brazilian prison was thwarted—by his own appetite.

Nineteen-year-old Leire Pereira Melo and his cellmate decided they'd had enough of life behind bars, so they decided to fly the coop—by using one of the iron bars that imprisoned them.

After several exhausting days, the inmates were able to wrench loose one of the solid rods from their cell door at a state prison in Goiania. Then, using the bar as a digging instrument, they burrowed a hole through the prison wall.

Melo's partner—who wasn't identified by authorities—easily wiggled through the hole and made good his escape. Melo, on the other hand, was a different story: Halfway through the makeshift passageway to freedom, he got stuck—and couldn't even work his way back *into* the cell.

Prison director Sidney Costa said guards found Melo a few hours later when they heard him screaming for help.

"He got stuck because he was a little on the chubby side, well, pretty fat, in fact," Costa said.

═════════

In March 1995, a twenty-six-year-old inmate walked away from his community work-release facility in South Carolina.

He was recaptured a week later when he went back to pick up his paycheck.

═════════

A twenty-seven-year-old prison escapee in San Mateo, California, was quickly recaptured after blowing his cover when he accidentally dialed 911.

Maliu Mafua—who was serving a six-month sentence for assault with a deadly weapon—somehow managed to walk away from a San Mateo minimum-security jail in January 1996. A short while later Mafua stopped at a pay phone in Los Altos, hoping to find someone to pick him up. Not having any phone numbers with him, Mafua attempted to call information to get a friend's phone number. But instead of dialing 411, the newly sprung jail-bird mistakenly dialed 911.

Mafua realized his error the second an emergency operator answered, so he quickly hung up without saying a word. What Mafua *didn't* realize, however, was that the Los Altos Sheriff's Department had a policy of following up on all 911 hang-ups.

When a patrol car arrived at the pay phone less than an hour later, the officers saw Mafua—still standing at the phone, and still wearing a shirt that had PROPERTY OF SAN MATEO COUNTY HONOR CAMP printed on the back in big, bold letters.

In January 1996 an Israeli judge rejected a prisoner's request to keep a blowup sex doll in his cell.

Prison guards seized the inflatable girlfriend from the cell of Amir Hazan, thirty-five, contending the doll could be used to hide contraband and weapons. They also feared if other prisoners borrowed it, the doll could be responsible for transmitting sexual diseases.

Hazan, who was imprisoned for "acts of violence," told the court he'd willingly give up his fight for the doll if prison officials would let him keep a real woman in his cell.

———

A man serving a twelve-year jail sentence in Kuwait found a meaty alternative to the prison's bland tofu patties: another inmate's nose.

The attack occurred after two inmates became involved in an argument. After biting off his fellow prisoner's nose, the sharp-toothed aggressor—whose name wasn't released—chewed up the schnozzola, so it couldn't be reattached by doctors.

Apparently, there was already bad blood between the two men. Earlier that day the biter taunted his victim by getting close to his face and barking like a dog.

———

A thirty-one-year-old inmate in Maine liked the food at the Rockland County Jail so much, he gained more than seventy pounds while waiting to be tried on robbery charges.

When Deane Brown's trial date finally came, guards brought him one of his outfits so he could change from the prison-issued jumpsuit to something more appropriate for court. The bloated Brown struggled to put on his pants, but it was no use—he couldn't even get them past his thighs.

Authorities were forced to postpone Brown's trial to a later date. And that was just fine with Brown, who was able to go back to scarf down more prison cuisine.

"It's all good, but if I had to pick one thing, I'd say the manicotti is the best," the 310-pound Brown told a local newspaper.

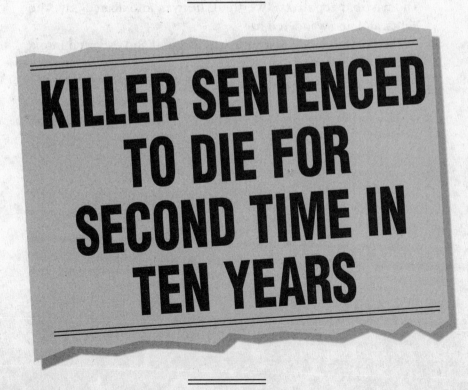

KILLER SENTENCED TO DIE FOR SECOND TIME IN TEN YEARS

A wrong-way burglar in Florida couldn't have made the police department's job any easier—he was arrested after breaking into the Glades Correctional Institution.

Police said Israel Martinez, twenty, was probably intoxicated when he jumped a fence, broke a screen, and climbed through a prison window in August 1995. Assistant superintendent Adam Thomas told reporters, "We think he was intoxicated, saw the lights, and just wandered in."

The dumbfounded Martinez was arrested and escorted into a cell.

CHAPTER VII

KNUCKLEHEADS ON THE JOB

Another story of a postal worker freaking out: On December 12, 1995, employees at the Postal Service terminal annex in Denver, Colorado, told police they became "concerned" when coworker John Pitney reported for work wearing a dress and carrying weapons. The fifty-year-old postal clerk was given the day off and escorted from the facility.

Later that same day Pitney—who had worked at the facility for five years—returned, apparently upset over his earlier dismissal. But this time, in addition to the dress and weapons, he was wearing a gorilla mask and a "strap-on sexual device."

His colleagues called the police, who arrested Pitney and charged him with disturbing the peace, trespassing, and making threats. Upon searching Pitney's pickup truck, officers found a high-powered rifle, two hunting knives, and the rest of his gorilla suit.

"The whole thing is absolutely shocking," one of the shaken employees later told reporters. "None of us can figure out where he got the gorilla suit from."

———

On January 19, 1996, members of the Royal Canadian Mounted Police kicked in the door of a suburban Vancouver home. After pulling the residents out of their beds, the raiding officers handcuffed them, forced them to the floor, and pointed guns at their heads.

Then they realized they had apprehended the wrong people.

Police Inspector Jim Good later told reporters he understood why the family was upset. "Guns were pointed, and this probably would have been perceived by them as a rough entry," he said.

———

It's a scene that's frustrated motorists ever since production of the Model T began in 1913: miles of congested traffic due to road construction, while idle city laborers stand around, apparently doing nothing.

In Romania, the government—up to their ears in complaints from disheveled drivers—decided to put an end to the negligence. After cruising past a group of alleged workers who were leaning on their shovels, a Transylvanian official came up with what he thought was a simple yet effective solution: shorten the handles.

Mayor Gheorghe Funar said the proposal was supposed to stop the "present working system where one man works while another ten colleagues and bosses watch, comment, and advise.

"The handles should be shortened so that they can no longer be used as a leaning point by those who meditate while at work," Funar said.

While the plan was a hit with the public, the shortened shovels proved to be a pain to workers—literally. The new, improved handles meant they were forced to bend over more when they *were* working, generating complaints of back trauma and accelerated exhaustion.

Before long, however, the lazy laborers discovered their new shovels weren't that bad: The next time Funar drove down the same stretch of crowded roadway, he caught the same workers slacking off again.

Only this time they were *sitting* on their shovels.

In October 1995 a Cambodian radio personality named Chiang Goan survived a hundred-foot fall from a tower. He credited the miracle to his lucky goat charm, which was strung around his neck at the time.

Bragging about the power of the charm to his listeners, Goan invited a soldier down to the station to fire a shot at him. Goan died instantly.

At least fourteen people were killed, thirty people were injured, and several roads and buildings were damaged when a truckload of explosives blew up while workers unloaded it.

The blast happened on January 14, 1996, in Sichuan, a province of China. Shipping employees were painstakingly unloading a ton of explosives, 5,000 detonators, and more than 1,500 feet of fuse when night fell upon the quiet region. Having no flashlights handy, the resourceful crew lit several candles to help them see while they finished their task.

The earth-shaking explosion occurred minutes later.

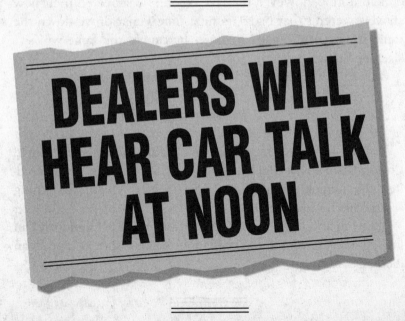

New York City has produced some pretty incredible Knuckleheads over the years, but none as surprising as Wall Street banking executive Gerard Finneran.

On October 20, 1995, the fifty-eight-year-old Greenwich, Connecticut, man was charged with assaulting several flight attendants and *defecating on a service cart* while returning from a business trip to Argentina.

The trouble began when flight attendants in first class refused to serve Finneran—who was described as "very intoxicated"—any more drinks. Outraged, he told one flight attendant he was going to "bust his ass," pushed another flight attendant into a seat, and started helping himself to the little liquor bottles from the service cart.

When the captain threatened to have him arrested, Finneran climbed on top of the cart, dropped his pants and underwear, and took a dump *in full view of the passengers.* To make matters worse, he grabbed a handful of linen napkins and proceeded to wipe himself.

According to one of the flight attendants, "there was poop everywhere. He tracked it through the aisle and smeared it all over the seats."

After completing the disgusting deed, the Air Force veteran and respected authority on Third World debt returned to his seat, covered himself with a blanket, and went to sleep.

Despite all the witnesses, Finneran pleaded "Not guilty" at his arraignment and was released on $100,000 bail—but only after promising to get the judge's permission before boarding another flight. His attorney told reporters, "He vigorously denies the allegations and expects an early and favorable resolution."

By the time his court date rolled around, Finneran's attorney had apparently struck a deal with prosecutors. The Wall Street bigwig pleaded guilty to misdemeanor assault charges for his run-in with the flight crew. His unscheduled pit stop on the service cart wasn't mentioned.

When Magistrate Steven Gold asked if he told a flight attendant he was going to "bust his ass," Finneran said, "I became annoyed and said words that implied a physical threat. I was angry."

Gold ordered Finneran to pay the airline $49,029 in restitution—$1,000 to clean up the airplane and the rest to reimburse the rest of the passengers for their inconvenience.

Afterward, Finneran's lawyer told reporters his client was a "marvelously decent human being" who had flown more than five million miles without any trouble. "He's not a man with a problem," he said.

As for defecating on the service cart, the attorney would only say Finneran had been suffering from an intestinal illness that led to diarrhea.

———

It takes plenty of brains, experience, and know-how to be a professional scientist. But in some cases, that just isn't enough.

After spending two years and more than $7 million on an antimissile satellite, a team of scientists from Russia and Utah State University were bewildered when it broke down after only one day in orbit.

Embarrassed USU staffers set out to determine the cause of the malfunction, and after several days of toiling over blueprints and walking through the assembly process again, they finally figured it out: The Russians wired a battery charger backward.

One of the USU scientists explained, "It's always the simple stuff that kills you."

————

In Rio de Janeiro, Brazil, circus goers are still mourning the loss of a king—"the *Fat* King."

For nine years 572-pound Reinaldo de Carvalho had been the main attraction at Rio's annual carnival. Then, in 1994, someone called him "Fatso" during his dance routine. Suffering from an acute case of bruised pride, Carvalho decided to knock off half the weight and he entered a diet clinic. After thirty days and 66 pounds, the Fat King keeled over, dead.

It took ten firefighters to carry him out, and the mortuary had to construct a special coffin from a piano box.

————

Taking into account the hordes of groupies, millions of dollars, and otherwise unobtainable perks associated with being a celebrity, referring to a successful career in the music industry as a "job" is enough to make your average Joe risk choking to death on his own words.

But to those who've worked all their lives for their place in the spotlight, the constant stress brought on by grueling tour schedules and demanding record companies, and overly obsessed fans can start to wear thin after a while. Before celebrities know it, their so-called glamorous lifestyles seem no better than the jobs they fought so desperately to get away from. Detestably *high-paying* jobs, but jobs nonetheless.

John Tesh should know. That is, if he thinks and feels like human beings do.

You see, according to the National Anti-Tesh Action Society, there's more to the entertainment-show-host-turned-dulcet-melody-maker than meets the eye. *Much* more.

According to the society's members, John Tesh is an alien.

No, not the kind that illegally slips past Arizona border officials in the soft light of the Mexican moon. The group believes that behind Tesh's all-American looks and squeaky clean image lies a cleverly disguised creature from the deepest regions of outer space. And, despite his former TV show's recognizable logo, E.T. he ain't.

While picketing one of Tesh's concerts in Detroit, Michigan, well-wishing Anti-Teshers handed out fliers revealing the inheritor of Yanni's throne as an "interplanetary mole" for the alien army Echelon.

When Tesh caught wind of the preconcert demonstration, he decided to take a shot at defusing the situation with a little light-hearted jocularity. He obtained the services of a photographer and raced outside, hoping to get together with his antagonists for a group shot.

Don't look for the picture on the cover of his next album, though. Upon seeing the lumbering pianist dashing toward them, the protesters began screaming and ran off.

One can only assume Tesh used some sort of Echelon mind-altering ray on the unfortunate bunch. The National Anti-Tesh Action Society hasn't been heard from since.

———

Rule number one when visiting a structurally unsound building: Wear a hard hat.

Perhaps the instructor of a safety seminar in Hennef, Germany, hadn't gotten to that one before his students were unexpectedly dismissed.

In the midst of a lecture on vocational hazards, students at the Academy for Workplace Safety found themselves running for cover when the ceiling suddenly collapsed. The barrage of falling plaster resulted in twelve injuries and the cancellation of the seminar.

———

Who says accountants are boring?

In May 1996 three women charged executives at a respected Wall Street accounting firm with sexual harassment, claiming they ran a Long Island branch like an unruly college frat house.

In the suit, the women—two former employees and one current worker—said they were subjected to foul language, intimidation, and lewd physical and verbal advances.

Among their claims against the branch manager:

- The manager created what they referred to as a "Boom-Boom Room" in the office's basement, complete with toilet bowel that was suspended from the ceiling and an oversized garbage can, from which the manager would ladle out Bloody Marys to male workers.
- He told one female employee she "should be hit by a bus."
- After detailing his plans to hire a Playboy bunny, the manager said he wanted to run a "whorehouse" from the office, ban women from golf outings, and hire masseuses to service male employees.
- Taking a cue from the Anita Hill–Clarence Thomas sexual harassment case, he shouted across the office, "I left a pubic hair on my Coke can!"

KNUCKLEHEAD IN THE SPOTLIGHT

PUTTING HIS BEST BIGFOOT FORWARD

Al Magnusson. He's a man who wears many hats. There's Al Magnusson the Party Animal. Al Magnusson the Organizer. Al Magnusson the Fighter of City Hall. And Al Magnusson the Bigfoot Lover.

Magnusson, who lives in the desolate Washington State community of Glacier, has been butting heads with the big boys at city hall over a gun-control issue that's near and dear to his heart: He wants to outlaw Bigfoot hunting.

"There's no proof that Bigfoot has ever done anything wrong," Magnusson said. "Why should it be legal for people to roam around in Bigfoot territory taking pot shots at them?"

Magnusson's passion for his work runs deeper than his love for eight-foot-tall hair-covered beasts. As a recognized community leader, he was burdened by his peers with the responsibility of organizing some sort of annual event that would help put Glacier on the map.

So, naturally, he came up with the Glacier Bigfoot Festival.

"Our first one was an incredible event," Magnusson said. "We had music, food, dancing, a Bigfoot foot competition, a parade, and, of course, a Bigfoot look-alike contest."

While the festival seemed like the perfect solution to his community's public-relations quandary, Magnusson said potential Bigfoot look-alike contestants had *cold* big feet when it came to entering the competition. With so many trigger-happy Sasquatch hunters roaming the foothills of neighboring Mount Baker, there was no telling what would happen to the group of bogus Bigfeet that were expected to conglomerate in Glacier.

"I mean, it's bad enough to shoot at poor creatures who keep to themselves," Magnusson explained. "But now we're talking about men with families and productive lives."

As a result, the voting public wasn't offered much of a selection when the time came to crown Glacier's foremost pseudo Sasquatch—the ballot listed only one candidate, who ended up winning by a landslide.

Magnusson, who admits he's never actually seen one of the festival's honorees, said the victor "didn't look much like Bigfoot. He did have a beard, though, and I guess he was kind of hairy."

Undaunted, the respected activist vowed to continue his struggle to keep America's most elusive creature off the endangered species list.

"Just because you don't see a lot of 'em doesn't mean their lives aren't worth anything," Magnusson said. Getting a far-off look in his eyes, he added, "One day, we'll have a Bigfoot festival and a whole lot of people who look like a Bigfoot will be there. You'll see."

CHAPTER VIII

KNUCKLEHEADS AND THEIR ANIMAL FRIENDS

For hundreds of years hunting dogs have fallen victim to misfired shots at the hands of their masters. But on January 22, 1996, a canine named Rusty finally got revenge.

Forty-five-year-old Phillip Smith was hunting birds in Inez, Kentucky. After Smith downed one of his feathered victims, Rusty—a fifteen-month-old cocker spaniel—retrieved the bird and brought it back to his master. The dog was reluctant to turn the prey over, however, so Smith set his rifle on the ground and tried to yank the bird out of Rusty's mouth. During the struggle to separate dog and bird, Rusty accidentally stepped on the trigger, shooting Smith in both legs.

"It's not funny that the guy got shot," said Martin County Sheriff Darriel Young. "But it's kind of funny *how* he got shot."

———

In Old Bridge Township, New Jersey, Eugene Octtaviano was charged with several counts of animal cruelty after police found four hundred birds living in his apartment.

Police raided Octtaviano's apartment after receiving numerous calls from his neighbors, who complained about a terrible odor and an overabundance of insects coming from the man's apartment. When they opened the door, officers found four hundred birds flying around the room—and dozens of unhatched eggs.

"The entire apartment's floor was covered an inch deep in feces and bird feed," Sgt. John Amabile said. "There were fifteen to twenty of them on each lamp, light fixture, and telephone."

Octtaviano explained the situation by saying, "I started out with a few birds, and I guess it got out of hand."

———

Every now and then an airplane is forced to make an emergency landing because the pilot miscalculates his remaining fuel supply. An aircraft that's forced to turn around because it has *too much* gas is almost unheard of.

But in April 1995 that's exactly what happened. A jumbo jet bound for South Africa had to retrace its course and make an emergency landing after a cargo of pigs had a gas attack.

The plane—which was carrying 300 passengers and 72 prize stud pigs—made an unscheduled landing at London Heathrow after the animals' uncontrollable flatulence, excessive urine, and body heat triggered the fire alarm.

Fifteen of the pigs, which were being flown to South Africa for breeding purposes, died of asphyxiation when halon gas was automatically released in the cargo hold to help put out the alleged fire.

SQUAD HELPS DOG BITE VICTIM

=====

In a newspaper column that appeared in the *Chicago Tribune*, movie critic Roger Ebert reviewed an animated Japanese movie called *Pompoko*.

Although the movie is about a gaggle of cute, furry badgers, Ebert didn't think it would be very successful in America. The badgers' secret weapon is an ability to make their testicles grow large so that they can crush opponents.

The kids in Japan think the secret weapon is "hilarious."

=====

Police in Bethel Park, Pennsylvania, arrested a man after he admitted having a sexual relationship with a dead, headless deer.

On December 6, 1996, Bethel Park police received several complaints of a "foul odor" emanating from a suburban Pittsburgh condominium. Upon entering the condo in question, officers had no trouble locating the source of the smell: a rotting, decapitated deer, which the resident had illegally killed with a crossbow.

The man—whose name wasn't released—was arrested and charged with deviant sexual intercourse. In addition to having sex with the animal, the man also told police that he drank its blood.

=====

In Cairo, Egypt, six people drowned when they tried to save a chicken that had fallen into a well.

According to the daily newspaper *al-Ahram*, the incident occurred in July 1995 after a chicken accidentally tumbled into a farmer's well in the village of Nazlet Emara, in the province of Sohag.

Upon discovering the mishap, the farmer's eighteen-year-old son jumped into the well in an effort to save the chicken. His good intentions went astray, however, and he drowned.

Realizing it was too late to save their brother, the teen's siblings—his two brothers, ages 20 and 16, and his sister, 14—jumped in one after the other, all hoping to save the chicken. All three met the same fate as their brother.

Two neighbors heard the commotion and rushed over and tried to save the kids. They also drowned.

The chicken was unharmed.

═══════════

When patrolman James Myers saw a pickup speed out of a parking lot without any lights on, he thought he had another drunk driver on his hands.

So the Urichsville, Ohio, officer flicked on the red-and-blues, radioed headquarters, and began following the erratically driven vehicle. But his efforts to maintain law and order in his otherwise quiet community were in vain; the driver of the truck refused to pull over.

With lights and siren blaring, Myers stayed behind the pickup as it turned onto a city street, ran over a median, and went four-wheeling across a resident's lawn. Then, after narrowly missing a house and a parked car, the out-of-control vehicle bounced through a ditch and eventually came to a stop in a muddy cornfield.

Myers, ready for a confrontation, cautiously approached the truck. But instead of finding an intoxicated, belligerent person behind the wheel, he was greeted by an overfriendly, ecstatic *dog*.

Brett Donohue, the owner of the pickup, later told police the dog wasn't even his. Apparently, the medium-sized, black-and-white collie was a stray and Donohue picked it up because he felt sorry for it. According to police reports, Donohue had left the engine running while he ran into a store for some beer . . . and he left the collie behind to discourage potential thieves from stealing his truck.

———

In Nairobi, Kenya, police arrested a middle-aged man after he broke into a glass case at a toy store and started strangling the stuffed lion that was inside.

When questioned by police, the man explained that his brother had been killed by a lion and he wanted revenge.

———

As long as anyone can remember, dogs have held the honorable distinction of being "man's best friend."

But more and more these days, some men have been replacing their canine companions with cows. In fact, they've been replacing their *women* with cows, too. A few cases from 1995:

In New Holland, Pennsylvania, police responded to a report that an intruder had broken into a local barn. When they burst in, investigating officers found fifty-five-year-old Jimmy Hutson—wearing nothing but tennis shoes—making mad, passionate love to a cow.

The naked Hutson made a dash for the barn's back door, but New Holland police officer Irvin Martin was waiting for him on the other side. Hutson was arrested and charged with deviate sexual intercourse and criminal trespass.

———

A twenty-eight-year-old man on trial in Zimbabwe told a judge he had sex with his cow because he was afraid of contracting AIDS from a human partner.

Israel Zinhanga, who lives in the small town of Rusape, also told the court he was in love with the cow, and went as far as to recite marriage vows to a picture of the animal as he stood before the judge.

The magistrate didn't buy into Zinhanga's romantic notions, however. Calling the case "abominable," he sentenced the man to nine months in jail. As police led Zinhanga out of the courtroom, he pledged to be faithful to the cow while serving his time.

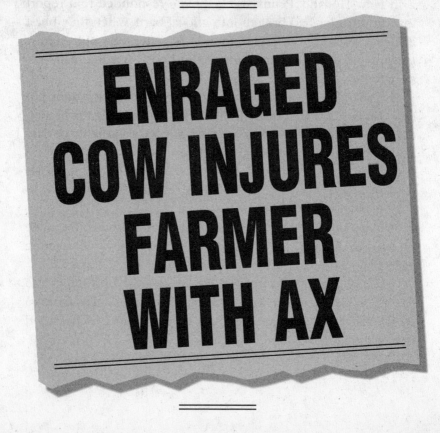

ENRAGED COW INJURES FARMER WITH AX

In Decorah, Iowa, a fifty-six-year-old man was accused of committing a sex act with a heifer at the Winneshiek County Fairgrounds.

Charles Starks, of Mabel, Minnesota, was visiting some friends in Iowa when he allegedly made a new friend in a barn at the fairgrounds. Although witnesses claimed they saw Starks making love to a cow, he maintained his innocence, claiming he'd only "urinated on them."

———

In 1939 the *Boston Globe* ran a story about a Harvard University student who swallowed a live goldfish to win a ten-dollar bet. Before long, thousands of crazy college kids were downing the slimy little creatures in hopes of gaining acceptance into prestigious fraternities and sororities all over the country. Naturally, the art of goldfish-swallowing isn't without its risks: Even today you occasionally hear of a student who was cut down in the prime of life because he couldn't handle his fish. It's a common and accepted risk.

But in July 1996 a Brazilian fisherman carved his own niche in fish-swallowing history by becoming the first person to choke to death on a fish that *voluntarily entered his mouth*.

Nathon do Nascimento was relaxing on the shore of the Maguari River, about thirty miles south of Belem, Brazil. After dropping his line in the water, Nascimento kicked back and watched his bobber sway back and forth atop the mesmerizing current. He leaned back and let out a long, relaxed yawn.

Big mistake.

At that moment a six-inch-long fish suddenly leapt from the river and soared between the boundaries of Nascimento's outstretched lips. It became lodged in his throat.

Unable to breath, the panic-stricken Nascimento started flopping around like—well, like a fish out of water. This attracted the attention of two other fishermen, who rushed to his aid. Attempts to remove the fish were unsuccessful, though; the good Samaritans couldn't reach the kamikaze fish's tail.

Nascimento was pronounced dead on arrival.

THE KING IS DEAD, LONG LIVE THE KNUCKLEHEADS

Elvis Presley was a god.

That statement rings true for millions of Elvis fans worldwide. But according to the way Stephanie G. Pierce sees things, such a comment would be nothing more than a flat-out insult. To Pierce, the late King of Rock 'n' Roll wasn't *a* god. Elvis *is* God.

Pierce is the self-proclaimed celebrity spokesmodel–minister of the 24-Hour Church of Elvis in Portland, Oregon.

"We're the first full-profit, full-service church that worships who should be worshiped," Pierce said. "I'm just answering my calling."

The Church of Elvis offers most of the services a traditional church would bequeath: wedding ceremonies, catechisms, communions, confessions, and daily sermons. Not to mention, of course, the traditional "photo opportunity with the King."

"We've got a cardboard cutout of him," Reverend Pierce explained. "It's life-sized and looks pretty real in photographs."

Pierce, an actual ordained minister who takes her profession quite seriously, said wedding ceremonies make up ninety percent of the church's most-requested services.

"If you can't afford the money for a full-blown wedding, we also offer a coin-operated wedding chapel that costs a dollar," she said, adopting a tone that would make even the most proficient used–pink Cadillac salesman proud. "You just drop your money in the slot and you're married. A marriage certificate comes out and everything. The problem is, that method isn't exactly legal. The regular way is legal, though."

Nevertheless, the coin-operated system has become so popular, Pierce has been forced to increase the automated Elvis services by two. One of the newest contraptions prints out psychic predictions, while the other—which is meant for use at Christmastime—dispenses holiday greetings.

Still, Pierce said, the Elvis wedding chapel remains the attraction's biggest draw.

"Elvis is such a big part of our everyday lives, it's no surprise we get people from all over who want to get married in his presence," she said. "I mean, who's better than Elvis to be part of a holy union between two people who love each other?"

Despite the church's eternal devotion to the bloated one, Pierce said wiggly-legged lovebirds scheduled to be married in the chapel shouldn't expect the *real* Presley to attend.

"We haven't seen him in a couple of weeks," she said.

CHAPTER IX

KNUCKLEHEADS IN LOVE

When it comes to lovemaking, there are moaners and there are screamers. After mistaking the sound of her oldest child's sexual shrieks for cries for help, a woman in Devizes, England, picked up the phone and got local police on the case.

The incident occurred in the wee hours of July 2, 1995. The mother of two was sound asleep when she was snapped out of her slumber by a ringing phone. Upon answering it, she was greeted by moans, groans, and yelling. The woman dismissed the call as a prank and hung up.

A short while later the phone rang again. This time the woman heard outright *screaming*, following by a female shouting, "Oh my God!" Terrified, the woman hung up. There was no mistaking it: The voice on the other end of the line belonged to her daughter, who lived about a hundred miles away.

The woman frantically called the police, who dispatched several squad cars to her daughter's home. After breaking down the door and storming into the bedroom, officers found the daughter—stark naked—making love to her boyfriend on the bed.

Apparently, during two wild moments of passion, the daughter's big toe accidentally hit the speed dial button on the phone, which was on a nightstand next to the bed.

"This is a warning for other people," a police spokesman said. "If you're going to indulge in that sort of thing, move the phone."

———————

A fetish for obese women and an insatiable appetite for alcohol proved to be a lethal combination for a West Palm Beach couple.

Two-hundred-seventy-pound Violia Thompson killed her 140-pound boyfriend when she accidentally fell on him and crushed him to death.

According to a police report filed in August of 1995, Thompson, thirty-nine, had been drinking with forty-eight-year-old August Grant when the accident occurred. After consuming an "inordinate amount" of alcohol, Thompson passed out and collapsed right on top of her diminutive lover. Several hours later she woke up and found Grant facedown on the bed, passed out in a pool of blood.

Thompson called an ambulance, but it was too late—her boyfriend was already dead.

A Kuwait man was rushed to hospital with back pain and exhaustion after making love to his seventeen-year-old wife six times a day during the week after their wedding.

The Kuwaiti newspaper *al-Watan* reported: "He was pale and powerless and could not speak. He had to be carried to an ambulance on the shoulders of friends. He felt dizzy and had excruciating pain in his back, and then collapsed in the living room."

A man who was golfing at a Stamford, Connecticut, golf course received quite a surprise when he went to retrieve a ball he had sliced into the woods. There, lying in a clearing, was a stocky man with his pants pulled down around his ankles—making mad, passionate love to a blowup doll.

Forgetting about his lost ball, the man quickly reported the golf course Casanova to a Parks and Recreation Department employee. The worker went to investigate, but all he saw was a suspicious-looking man leaving the course, carrying a brown gym bag.

The unwilling Peeping Tom described the man as white, unshaven, in his mid-thirties or early forties, and wearing a blue sweatshirt and jeans. He was unable to provide police with a description of the blowup doll.

A Russian couple trying to integrate a few American traditions into their marriage apparently took the Yankee phrase "tough love" a bit too literally.

After exchanging vows in June 1994, the newlyweds cut their wedding cake and proceeded to scoop up two generous pieces with the intent of feeding each other. As a gaggle of family members gathered around and readied their cameras, the overzealous bride—who had evidently overindulged during the champagne toast—cocked back her arm and stuffed the frosting-covered slice into her mate's mouth. Suddenly, a resounding "snap" echoed through the reception hall—the man's jaw had been broken.

The groom was taken to a hospital in the Siberian city of Barnaul, where doctors wired his fractured snout shut.

"It was his idea to do it," a relative told reporters. "It wasn't her fault. She was just in a hurry to get it over with."

━━━━━━

In March 1996 a woman with a handsome bank account decided to test her boyfriend's pledge of eternal love . . . so she made up a story about having $741,000 stolen to see if he'd stay with her even if she had no money.

To make the fabrication seem more believable, thirty-three-year-old Linda Kee called police and reported the bogus burglary. When officers arrived at the couple's Delaware home, they told her the FBI would have to be called in because of the amount of the theft. That's when she fessed up.

Apparently, her little prank didn't settle well with Delaware's boys-in-blue. They slapped her with a misdemeanor charge of filing a false police report.

On the up side, the couple ended up staying together.

"Apparently, he passed the test," Detective Mike Askew said.

In October 1995, police in Jefferson County, Missouri, charged Daniel Thomas with reckless driving after they caught him four-wheeling through a city councilman's prize rose garden.

When investigating officers asked the nineteen-year-old why he'd been driving so wildly, Thomas explained that he lost control of the vehicle when his girlfriend bit him while administering oral sex.

A woman in Kissimmee, Florida, should have no trouble remembering her new husband's name. But, following a bizarre chain of coincidences surrounding the couple's wedding, she *might* have trouble remembering what he looks like.

Ronald Legendre married his girlfriend, Hope, in August 1995. The best man—who wasn't related to the groom in any way—was *also* named Ronald Legendre. And the ceremony was performed by someone who wasn't connected to *either* man: Judge Ronald Legendre.

There's no word on what the Legendres plan to name their firstborn son.

═══════════

It can get awfully lonely in prison. Just ask thirty-two-year-old Sheila Tavarez.

When the 275-pound woman was released from a Florida detention facility in March 1994, Tavarez had only one thing on her mind: to make up with her estranged boyfriend, who had dumped her when she was incarcerated.

After receiving her personal belongings from a prison clerk, the Miami Beach woman immediately drove to the convenience store where her former lover worked. She begged for a reconciliation, but her pleas fell upon deaf ears—the man wanted nothing to do with her.

Outraged by the rejection, Tavarez picked up the thirty-four-year-old man and threw him into a walk-in cooler, where he landed on a case of bottled beer. Then she plucked him from the briny of broken glass and tore off his smock—which she used to tie him up.

Pushing him to the floor again, the horny heavyweight took off her coat and sat on the unlucky man—refusing to get off until he agreed to go out with her. Two hours later the ex-con's ex finally gave in. After making arrangements to meet later that evening, Tavarez left for home to prepare for the date.

Sadly, the romantic encounter never happened. When Tavarez got home, she found two police officers—responding to her ex-boyfriend's call—waiting outside her door. Tavarez was arrested and charged with assault—less than four hours after her release from jail.

———————

The premise isn't new: couple has more and more trouble finding spark that once fueled relationship; husband becomes "distant," begins spending more time at the office; lonely house-wife resorts to illicit affair in an attempt to recapture the atten-tion formerly given by husband; husband finds out about it, files for divorce.

Thousands of couples fall victim to similar relationship-destroying events every year. But it's not the premise that earned John and Diane Goydan a place in Knucklehead history; credit the *details* of their well-publicized marital spat. When John went public with his wife's alleged affaire d'amour, the Goydans gave a whole new meaning to the term "long-distance relationship."

When the Bridgewater, New Jersey, man discovered his spouse was having cybersex with a mysterious on-line partner, he sued her for divorce, claiming an affair is an affair, whether it's physi-cal or virtual.

The history-making case hatched in late 1995 when Diane—apparently dissatisfied with her hubby's contributions to the relationship—discovered an area on America On-Line called

"Married but Looking." It was there that she met her knight in shining armor—an unidentified North Carolina man who frequented the site under the screen name the "Weasel."

"[John] became distant and removed from her," Diane's lawyer, Thomas McCormick, told reporters, "which may have led to her going on-line."

After dozens of sexually explicit on-line conversations, Diane and her appropriately named virtual lover—who was also married—decided to consummate the relationship at a New Hampshire bed and breakfast. The unintentionally befitting date for the intimate encounter with the Weasel: Groundhog Day, 1996.

The clandestine liaison wasn't meant to be, however. One day, while browsing various web sites on the couple's home computer, John inadvertently stumbled upon his wife's used letter file. Unable to resist the temptation, he scrolled through the personal documents. The text read like a "best of" compilation from the pages of *Penthouse Forum*.

On January 23, 1996, the distraught Mr. Goydan made it official: He filed divorce papers charging his wife with adultery. Among other things, he sought custody of their children, a seven-year-old girl and a three-year-old boy.

Speaking through her attorney, the red-faced Diane called the adultery charges "ludicrous," characterizing the correspondence as nothing more than harmless "daydreams." Furthermore, she accused her husband of violating state wiretap laws by delving into her personal documents, claiming e-mail should be protected by the same laws that guard what net-heads refer to as "snail mail."

"My client is devastated by the allegation of adultery, that I believe is without basis in law or fact," McCormick said. "It was something she had every right to expect to remain private."

Soon, reporters from all over the world had congregated around the couple's quiet suburban home, writing stories that carried headlines like MAN SEEKS DIVORCE FROM CYBERSLUT and ANGRY CYBERSEX WIFE DOWNLOADS ON HUBBY. Before long Diane was promising a lawsuit of her own, accusing her estranged partner of sticking a well-sharpened barb into her hard drive by sharing the woeful tale with anyone and everyone carrying a reporter's notepad. She referred to John's actions as "extreme cruelty."

Although the Weasel presumably emerged from the scandal unscathed, don't expect the mysterious cyberjunkie to board the P.C. to passion anytime soon. A recent check of his screen name resulted in the following message: "Not a known user."

━━━━━

Even at the ripe old age of 79 a Michigan Romeo has still got it.

Not that he really wants it.

Macomb Township resident John Papuga filed stalking charges against his eighty-year-old widowed neighbor, charging the elderly woman with vigilantly pursuing his affections over a three-year period.

The geriatric gigolo says the unwelcomed courtship began when Frances Breiholz saw him wearing a red hat. For some reason, the sight of his crimson lid turned the woman into a love-crazed bull on an unbridled mating mission, and she began leaving him notes, whispering sweet nothings over the phone, blowing him kisses, and propositioning him whenever he ventured outside.

Breiholz denied the allegations, telling police Papuga was a few bricks shy of a load. She said she sent him a letter about four years before the charges were filed, and the closest thing she'd ever done to "propositioning" him was offer a friendly wave whenever he walked by.

The case was still in dispute at press time. If convicted, Breiholz faces up to a year behind bars and a thousand-dollar fine.

STUD TIRES OUT

LOONEY AND THE BEASTS

When Cossette Willoughby took up the challenging sport of rock hunting, she had no idea she'd end up making loads of new friends.

Although the seventy-seven-year-old Las Cruces, New Mexico, woman seems perfectly capable of holding lengthy conversations with the rocks she collects, Willoughby claims her freshly acquired companions are very much alive—in the form of Tasmanian Devil–like creatures that disappear and reappear on command.

"I'm still afraid to walk too close to them, but I'm pretty sure they like me," Willoughby said. "I make them feel safe."

Willoughby, who first discovered the creatures while stalking stones near her trailer park, said each stands about six feet tall and is covered with short, coarse, black hair.

"I was looking for some nice rocks when I saw a group of them standing on a small hill," she explained. "At first, I thought they were bears. All of a sudden they noticed me and faded into the darkness. They just disappeared."

Since that time, Willoughby has cemented her friendship with the beasts by bringing them gifts.

"They like candy very much," she said. "So I leave them little bags of it. They take it and eat it up right away. Once I even left them a little mirror in one of the bags. The next night, I was looking through my window, and I saw a light shining outside. I knew they were playing with the mirror I left them."

After her initial offering, Cossette's pals reciprocated by leaving her small handmade amulets in an easy-to-find location: strewn about the desert area where she hunts for rocks.

Since then Willoughby has collected dozens of the amulets, which she'll gladly show anyone who asks. She claims the charms bear likenesses of snakes and serpents—but others might see a closer resemblance to, well, rocks.

Although she has never actually spoken to the mysterious animals, Willoughby said they once tried to communicate with her.

"The door of my trailer was opened a little and I heard a little voice saying, 'Cossette . . . Cossette . . . Cossette,' " she said. "I tried to close the door, but I could feel a hand holding it open. A furry hand."

Willoughby's not the only Las Cruces resident to have encountered the unidentified species. Her husband, Paul, saw one while waiting for his wife to return from rock hunting.

"He was sitting in the car on the side of the road, when suddenly he saw a big whirlwind—like a little tornado—go by the front of the car," she said. "He knew right then it was one of them."

Willoughby admitted she hasn't encountered the hairy monsters in a few months.

"I hurt my leg, so I haven't been out rock hunting lately," she said. "But then again, they haven't been by to see *me*, either."

CHAPTER X

KNUCKLEHEADS ON THE NET

Ken Osmond, the actor who played Eddie Haskell on *Leave It to Beaver*, grew up to become rock star Alice Cooper; Barry Williams, Greg from *The Brady Bunch*, kept his career alive by whipping out his little Sam the butcher in porn films; and John Gilcrest, the kid who played Mikey in those popular cereal commercials, met an untimely demise when a lethal combination of Pop Rocks and cola caused his stomach to explode.

Long before American homes were introduced to the gizmos, gadgets, bells, and whistles that fuel the computer age, these stories—and stories just like them—have shocked and intrigued people as they were passed along in high school hallways, employee cafeterias, and weekend get-togethers. Sure, they're fascinating. They're fun to tell. They procure everyone's attention. But, sadly and simply, they're not true.

They're called "urban legends."

Then home personal computers came along. Instead of innocently wandering onto the Information Superhighway, we blindly boarded a runaway train with an unquenchable thirst for faster gizmos, more impressive gadgets, and louder bells and whistles that trill Beethoven's Fifth in three different keys. As the unbridled locomotive thundered into the nineties, it inevitably picked up a few hermetic stowaways along the way. Stragglers in the human race who viewed the Internet as a soapbox where they could finally be heard by people who previously wouldn't give them the time of day, a grandstand where even the most demure shut-in could be a Bill Cosby in a world of Nipsey Russells.

Unfortunately, these stowaways really didn't have much to say. As a result, an increased volume of urban legends—both old and new—started popping up faster than ever before, replacing facts with distortions at every stop.

What follows is a collection of popular stories that have been floating around the Internet for the last few years. Since the original sources couldn't be tracked down, there's no way of knowing which stories are actually factual, which have been factually tweaked for the sake of entertainment, and which are out-and-out fiction. So, for safety's sake, the names of the involved parties have been changed.

Subj: Knucklehead Victims
Date: 95-09-14 15:28:38 EDT
From: Moe Demm@well.com (Morris K. Demm)
To: Katomac565@aol.com

It seemed like just another morning for Steven Turner.

After several ungrateful blows to the alarm clock's snooze button, Turner stumbled out of bed, shaved, got dressed, and poured a cup of high-petroleum java down his gullet. He completed his morning ritual by kissing his wife and heading out to the garage, where he expected his new Honda Accord to be waiting for him.

Upon raising the garage door, however, the Kansas City, Missouri, man discovered he'd had an uninvited visitor during the night. The car was *gone*.

After he broke the news to his wife, Tina, the violated couple filed a police report and an investigation was launched. A few days passed and Kansas City police were unable to come up with as much as a drop of oil from the hijacked Honda, so the Turners began fearing the worst: Either the car had been dismantled and parted out, or it was sporting a new paint job somewhere in Mexico.

Then, one afternoon, Tina opened the mailbox to find *another* surprise: an envelope from the thief.

In the neatly typed letter, the car-napper explained he had stolen the vehicle because his pregnant wife had gone into labor and required immediate hospitalization. He wrote he was "extremely sorry for the trouble" he'd caused, but promised to return the Honda as soon as his wife and new baby were released from the hospital.

The following morning, Steven abandoned his forenoon ritual, threw on a robe, and went straight to the garage. Sure enough, the car was back, parked in the exact spot it had been stolen from nearly a week before. Checking the interior for damage, Steven found a box of candy and two tickets to a sold-out stage show as retribution for the inconvenience. Looking forward to starting a family of their own, the Turners were touched by the crook's genuine remorse and told police the whole thing had been a big mix-up. The case was dropped.

The next night, a Friday, Steven and Tina climbed into their Accord and went to the show. Their seats were incredible and they had a night they wouldn't soon forget.

In more ways than one. When they returned home, the Turners opened their front door to find their house had been ransacked and more than $40,000 worth of jewelry, televisions, and other household goods had taken flight.

Secured to the wall unit was *another* note from the intruder: "I hope you enjoyed the show!"

Subj: Suicidal Tendencies
Date: 96-09-21 14:39:02 EDT
From: Meg Abyte@net.rjm.com (Abyte, Megan)
To: Katomac565@aol.com

A suicidal man apparently missed his mark when he jumped from a fifteenth-story window—but succeeded in getting his death wish when he was shot on the way down.

Mark Thompson, despondent over his dismal financial situation, decided to take his own life by leaping from a hall window in a high-rise apartment building in Chicago. So the unemployed factory worker scrawled out a suicide note, climbed through the window, and demonstrated his best cannonball off the ledge.

His abrupt meeting with Lake Shore Drive wasn't meant to be, however. Chronically afraid of heights, the thirty-two-year-old Thompson failed to look before he leaped; if he had, he would've noticed the net bordering the building's seventh floor, meant to protect two workers who were diligently washing the ninth-floor windows.

Under normal circumstances, the safety device would've thrown an industrial wrench into Thompson's efforts, but he was *saved*—for lack of a better word—by an elderly man who was arguing with his wife on the twelfth floor. At that exact moment, the man decided to end the altercation by firing a shotgun at his incensed spouse. Fortunately, again, for lack of a better word, the man's aim was as misguided as his judgment. The blast crashed through the window and struck Thompson, who happened to be falling by at the time.

As if the story isn't weird enough, Chicago police ended up charging the senior citizen with murder, reasoning Thompson would have lived if he'd been allowed to make it to the seventh-story net. The accused man claimed he was innocent, however, reasoning he *regularly* threatened his wife with a shotgun—but he never kept it loaded. Because the firearm had been loaded without his knowledge, the man felt Thompson's death should be ruled accidental.

The plot became thicker than Dom DeLuise's back hair when a witness came forward, stating she saw the couple's son loading the weapon about three weeks earlier. Apparently, the tapped-out couple threatened to cut off their son's financial support, so the disgruntled young man—who knew his dad liked to wave unloaded shotguns around—filled it with ammo to get revenge. Convinced by the eyewitness account, investigators decided to scratch the elderly man from their suspect list and instead charge his *son* with the crime.

But the son never even set foot in a courtroom, much less a prison cell. He turned out to be Mark Thompson, the guy who had jumped out of the fifteenth-story window in the first place.

The case was closed as a suicide.

Subj: Maid to Order
Date: 96-05-03 09:30:01 EDT
From: Mike Rosoft@sit.com
To: Katomac565@aol.com

The following transcription comes from a recording that was played during a murder trial in Oklahoma City, Oklahoma. Apparently, the answering machine had picked up just as the phone was answered, and the entire conversation was preserved for all to hear:

While at work, a man dialed his home number to talk to his wife. A strange woman answered the phone.

"Who are you?" he demanded.

"I'm the maid," the woman answered defiantly. "Who are *you*?"

"I'm the man of the house!" he responded. "And we don't have a maid!"

"I'm terribly sorry, sir," the flustered woman replied. "Your wife just hired me this morning."

"She *did*, did she? Where is she now?"

"Well, sir, I really shouldn't say."

"Is something wrong?"

"No, sir. It's just that . . . um, I really don't think it's my business."

"My wife might've hired you, but *I'm* the one paying your salary. I want to know where she is!"

Reluctantly, the maid said, "She's upstairs in the bedroom."

"Well, put her on the phone!"

"I can't."

"Why the hell not?"

"I don't want to start any trouble, sir."

Already suspecting his wife of being unfaithful, the man asked, "What? Is she with someone?"

After a pause, the woman said, "I naturally assumed he was her husband. How was I supposed to know?"

Hurt and outraged, the husband said, "How'd you like to make a little extra money? How does $75,000 sound?"

"It sounds great, but I don't understand what—"

"All you gotta do is get my gun and shoot 'em. Both of 'em."

"Are you crazy?"

"Listen. Where did my wife find you?"

"In the paper. She called yesterday."

"When did she hire you?"

"This morning. I came out for an interview and she hired me right away. She wanted me to start immediately."

"So nobody knew you took the job?"

"No. I don't think so."

"So, what do you have to lose? There's no way anyone would think you'd have something to do with it, because you supposedly don't know either of us. And I'll be okay because everyone sees me at work. It's an easy seventy-five grand."

Another pause. Finally, the woman said, "Where's the gun?"

"It's in a shoe box. On the top shelf of the coat closet right by the front door. Just put the phone down and do it now. Let me know what happened when you're through."

"Right now?"

"Right now. The closet by the front door."

The maid set the receiver on the table, and less than five minutes later the man heard screaming and three loud gunshots. After another five minutes had passed she finally got back on the line.

"Hello?" the frightened maid whispered, obviously upset by the ordeal.

"Did you do it?"

"Uh-huh," she said. "I had to shoot the man twice. He tried grabbing the gun."

"That son of a bitch," he growled, picturing the man he suspected of sleeping with his wife. "Now, try to stay calm. Everything's gonna be all right."

After making arrangements for the money to change hands, the maid asked, "Should I put the gun back in the shoe box?"

"No. Why don't you put it on the bedroom floor, next to the exercise bike? It'll look like someone broke in and used my gun to shoot her. And open up a couple drawers so they'll think someone was robbing us when they heard that bitch upstairs."

"I didn't see an exercise bike in your room."

"She must've moved it. Just leave it at the foot of the bed. And you know the door that leads out to the deck? Leave it open. The lock's already broken."

"What deck?"

"Uh, is this 555-2379?"

———————

Subj: Fwd: Time to "Change" Professions
Date: 95-02-09 16:09:44 EDT
From: Hugh Zerfrendly
To: Katomac565@aol.com

For all of us who scoffed at our high school arithmetic teachers when they said we'd need math skills later in life, consider the story of a half-witted holdup man in Arizona:

A man walked into a Tempe convenience store, slapped a twenty-dollar bill onto the counter, and asked for change. When the obliging clerk opened the cash register, the man pulled out a gun and demanded *all* the cash in the drawer—or else.

Finding new meaning in the word "oblige," the clerk promptly complied with the request, forking over every last cent of the store's monetary intake. The bandit scooped up the money and ran, leaving the twenty-dollar bill behind.

As it turned out, the part-time employee wouldn't have been able to give the thief change, anyway. The total amount stolen: $14.53.

———————

Subj: A Possible Explanation for the Bermuda Triangle
Date: 96-06-19 16:20:48 EDT
From: Doc U. Ment@inter.com (Dr. Upton Ment)
To: Katomac565@aol.com

Combine one part raging fires and one part monumental earthquakes in a valley-shaped bowel. Using a corrupt billy club, stir in massive flooding and discouraging crime statistics before sprinkling with riots. Cover entire mixture with blanket of smog and let simmer.

To some, the ingredients of Nostradamus's worst nightmare. To others, the recipe for another day in California.

Considering the mélange of tragedies that consistently plague the Golden State, you'd think its tireless emergency workers have seen it all. After extinguishing a fire that raged through one of Los Angeles County's remaining forests in early 1996, they probably *have*.

While assessing the damage caused by Mother Nature's latest temper tantrum, firefighters found a corpse in the middle of the woods. Although officials thought they'd thoroughly evacuated the area before the blaze could result in any casualties, this wasn't the reason they were so baffled by the discovery. Instead they found themselves scratching their heads over the dead man's apparel—an underwater wet suit, complete with an oxygen tank, face mask, and flippers.

Since there were no visible blisters on the body and the scuba tank had plenty of oxygen left, they were quick to rule out either burns or smoke inhalation as cause of death. Although a subsequent autopsy proved to be a success, the findings only *added* to the mystery. The mysterious stiff had died from internal injuries.

Investigators immediately embarked on a mission to make sense of the seemingly nonsensical tragedy. Once a check of his dental records unveiled the man's identity, they tracked down some of his friends and relatives and were able to piece together the following story:

On the day of the fire, the unlucky sap decided to seek refuge from the heat by going on a diving trip off the coast—at least twenty miles away from the fire. Meanwhile, back in the forest, frustrated firefighters were losing their battle against the searing flames. That's when they brought in the heavy artillery—a fleet of helicopters equipped with large-capacity water tanks, capable of dousing entire areas with swimming-pool-sized loads of H_2O.

Following regular procedure, the choppers flew out over the ocean and scooped up the desperately needed water. Unbeknownst to one volunteer pilot, his liquid cargo included the hapless diver, who was unintentionally sucked into the tank as he began to surface.

The confusion the unwilling passenger must have experienced as he soared through the air in the dark, steel-encased prison didn't last long, however. As soon as the helicopter was over its target, the pilot opened the hatch—and the diver was sent plummeting toward the inferno from a thousand feet in the air.

Forwarded Message:
Subj: Fwd: Employee Record
Date: 94-10-30 09:21:27 EDT
From: E. Mayle@pro.com (Eleanor Mayle)
To: Meg Ahertz@inter.com, Katomac565@aol.com

Allegedly, this is a real employee record posted by a personnel worker at a major clothing manufacturer:

Employee—Thomas Pickering
Date of Birth—08/02/54
Start Date—02/13/88
Termination Date—06/05/88

March 8—Tom vocalizes loud belch in employee cafeteria . . .

March 15—Tom disrupts lunch by noisily passing gas in employee cafeteria; belches while supervisor reprimands him . . .

March 16—Workday interrupted when Tom gets in loud argument with other employee . . . other employee says Tom belched in his face after saying, "Do you want some lunch?" Tom denies story . . .

April 3—Tom is observed passing gas into a telephone receiver during morning break . . .

April 28—Shipping clerk accuses Tom of wiping a piece of nasal discharge on his arm; Tom denies story, claims there was no nasal discharge on his finger when incident occurred . . .

May 10—Tom throws labeling gun across work area, nearly striking supervisor; says he was angry because said labeling gun wasn't working properly . . .

May 12—Tom loudly tells story of recent intestinal illness and messy results of said illness in employee cafeteria; makes inappropriate comment about coworker's weight . . .

May 13—Tom loudly tells inappropriate joke in employee cafeteria; is accused of telling said joke to "annoy" coworker mentioned in May 12 entry . . .

May 19—Tom uses his mouth to simulate sounds of passing gas on numerous occasions; accused other employees of passing gas . . .

May 20—Tom either naturally passes gas or simulates said gas sound when supervisor walks past his work station; when confronted, uses foul language and strongly suggests supervisor is "out to get" him . . .

May 23—Tom belches numerous times in employee cafeteria, claims he's "reciting the alphabet" . . .

June 2—Tom brags about visit to employee rest room . . . notes that he left toilet in said rest room unflushed . . .

━━━━━━

Subj: St. Tupperware's Day Massacre
Date: 94-04-12 15:55:12 EDT
From: Em Essdoss (Emily Essdoss)
To: Katomac565@aol.com

Canadian police were called to the home of Kelly Ross when a riot broke out at a party she was hosting. A *Tupperware* party.

According to the police report, two of the women began arguing over how to wash a deviled-egg tray in an automatic dishwasher. One of the women said it should be placed in the top rack so it wouldn't warp; the other contended it was perfectly fine to wash it in the bottom rack. Before long the other guests found themselves taking sides and a veritable cage match began. One Tupperware connoisseur smashed a lamp over another's head; one woman shoved another woman's face against the wall of the fireplace; another ripped a colleague's blouse off and doused her with fruit punch.

When it was all over, Ross was left with an estimated $12,000 damage to her house and three women were taken to the hospital—two for head injuries, the other for "multiple stab wounds."

Believe it or not, no one was arrested.

Forwarded Message:
Subj: Fwd: Dumb Ass Crooks
Date: 96-07-14 22:30:17 EDT
From: Win Doze@Stay.com (Winston R. Doze)
To: A. O. Ell, I. B. Emm, Katomac565@aol.com

In Little Rock, Arkansas, a gang of crooks pulled off what some consider to be impossible: They infiltrated a guarded savings bank, swiped more than $4,000 of its customers' money, and made their escape completely undetected.

And they did it without fancy gadgets or technical equipment. All they used was a felt-tipped marker and a plain cardboard box.

Scribbling "Night deposit box is broken, please deposit here" on the side of the box, the big thinkers left it before the *real* deposit box in the drive-through lane. Then they went about their business for the next few hours.

By the time they retrieved the box, dumb depositors had dumped $2,704 in cash and checks totaling $1,315 into the glaringly obvious replacement.

Subj: Check the Zapruder Film!!
Date: 96-01-11 10:38:44 EDT
From: SY NONN@badears.def.com
To: Katomac565@aol.com

While tooling down a highway in Lexington, Kentucky, a man became concerned as he watched the car in front of him violently swerve across the road and come to an abrupt stop on the shoulder. There was obviously something wrong with the driver.

The Good Samaritan pulled over, hopped out of his car, and hightailed it across the road. As he approached the driver's window he could make out a woman, hunched over the steering wheel, holding the back of her head.

As he got closer he could hear her scream, "I've been shot! I've been shot!"

The man opened the door and examined her head. No blood. He surveyed the interior of the car. No broken windows.

When he asked the woman to move her hands so he could get a better look at the wound, the woman flat-out refused, insisting her brains were falling out of the back of her head.

After several minutes of coaxing, the woman finally agreed to risk spilling her noodles. She raised her hands, revealing what very well *might* have been her brain—but in this case wasn't. Lazily hanging from the back of her head was an uncooked glob of biscuit dough.

The woman, who'd just finished grocery shopping, was on her way home with the bags on the backseat. Perched atop the heap of French pastries and diet soda was one of those little canisters that contain refrigerated pop-in-the-oven biscuits. For some reason the tube had accidentally exploded, firing the high-powered biscuit goo right into the back of her skull.

CHAPTER XI

KNUCKLEHEADS IN PAIN

Everyone knows that driving a small sports car can be dangerous, but nineteen-year-old Troy Harding has proved that *washing* one isn't always safe, either.

On May 29, 1995, the Portland, Oregon, resident was waxing his 1984 Pontiac Fiero when he somehow managed to shove the antenna *up his nose*. The thin metal rod punctured his sinus cavity and found its way to Harding's brain, where it struck his pituitary gland.

After losing more than a pint of blood, Harding was rushed to a Portland hospital. Amazingly, there was no brain damage, but he spent three weeks recovering from severe headaches and an inability to keep his balance.

Harding has since made a full recovery.

A twenty-two-year-old Seattle woman walked into the emergency ward at a Washington hospital, complaining of agonizing stomach pains. She told the attending physician she'd been suffering from nausea, vomiting, and a dull pain in her back for the past three weeks.

After examining the woman, doctors found the problem: She had a *tube sock* in her stomach.

The woman admitted that five months earlier she'd developed a nervous habit of eating about half a sock every night.

"Up until now, I haven't had any problems," she told the doctor.

DRUNK GETS NINE MONTHS IN VIOLIN CASE

Seventeen-year-old Kevin Hunt of London, England, is alive and well after undergoing surgery to remove a toothbrush from his stomach.

The mishap occurred in November 1995 when Hunt was getting ready for work. Short on time, Hunt tried to speed things along by simultaneously washing his hair and brushing his teeth while taking a shower. While rinsing the shampoo from his mane, Hunt clenched the toothbrush between his teeth and threw back his head to keep the soap suds from running into his eyes. Unfortunately, the tilting action caused some toothpaste to drip down his throat and Hunt began choking. Before he knew it, the six-inch toothbrush slipped down his gullet and became that morning's breakfast.

Believe it or not, Hunt did *nothing* to remedy the situation.

"I didn't know what to do, so I just carried on," he later told the *Sun* newspaper.

And carry on he did. After getting dressed, Hunt shuffled off to work and went about his normal activities as if nothing had ever happened. He didn't even bother telling his mother about the incident until some twenty-four hours later.

Finally, three days after ingesting the dental instrument, Hunt began to experience excruciating stomach pains. His mother rushed him to the hospital, where doctors put him under the knife to remove the toothbrush.

After surgery, Hunt showed off his surgical scar and posed for pictures with the toothbrush hanging out of his mouth.

"I told him it's just as well he didn't have an electric toothbrush," his mother told reporters.

―――――――――

On October 2, 1995, sixty-seven-year-old Domingo Morales stumbled into the emergency room at New York's Jacobi Hospital, complaining of a sharp pain between his legs. Upon examining Morales, doctors had no trouble pinpointing the reason for the retired truck driver's discomfort: His penis had been chopped off.

Police were called to the scene and Morales told them the sloppy circumcision was performed by a prostitute. Apparently, after receiving service from said prostitute, Morales refused to pay her exorbitant fee—so the Lorena Bobbit wannabe took a knife to his penis, keeping the dismembered organ as a souvenir.

In an effort to find the lopped-off digit while its nerves were still ripe, dozens of New York's Finest scoured Morales's Bedford Park neighborhood, but came up empty-handed. His wound was stitched shut and the press had a field day.

Now here's where the story gets *really* weird: The following day, Morales's brother stopped by his apartment to pick up a few things to make his sibling's hospital stay a little more pleasant. While doing so, he came across a Tupperware container, which had been stashed behind some cans on a kitchen shelf. It contained Morales's severed member.

Confronted with the discovery, Morales admitted that the prostitute story was a lie. An amateur guitar maker in his spare time, Morales was working on a new instrument in his underwear when the accident occurred.

"He had the neck of a guitar between his legs while he was working on it with a knife," Detective Frank Grecco said. "The knife slipped off the guitar and severed . . . his penis."

For some reason, Morales felt it would less embarrassing if he told police the slice-job came at the hands of a prostitute rather than his own. So he hid the bloody body part in a plastic container and went to the hospital.

Doctors tried to reattach the penis, but it was too late.

―――――――

In Tennessee, a senior citizen went to her doctor, complaining of a sharp pain in her buttocks. After taking X rays of the afflicted area, the doctor diagnosed the condition as a tumor and admitted her to the hospital to have it removed.

But when surgeons cut their patient open, they found the lump in her buttocks *wasn't* a tumor; it was a pork chop bone. She didn't remember sitting on it, but doctors estimated it had been jammed in there for five or ten years.

If you're going to end it all, you might as well go out with a roar.

That must've been what a Guatemala City resident was thinking when he decided life wasn't worth living anymore. So the thirty-five-year-old man drove to the National Zoo, scaled two towering fences, and dove head first into a *tiger cage*.

According to a spokesman for the zoo, the suicide victim made himself more appetizing by cutting his own neck before offering himself as the beasts' human du jour. Moments after he landed, the two ferocious tigers that call the enclosure "home" were on him like flies on manure.

As horrifying as the incident sounds, zoo officials should be used to things of that nature: Only a month earlier, *another* man killed himself at the National Zoo—by jumping into a jaguar cage.

———————

At one time or another, we've all been through the unpleasant childhood experience of staring at a nauseating plate of food while our mothers dutifully reminded us that millions of kids were starving in China.

If only we would've known the story of Zhao Jun.

On March 22, 1996, the Beijing man scored a victory for children all over the world when he *ate himself to death*.

Jun, a Beijing farmworker and apparent chain-smoker, got into an argument with a cohort over who could eat the most gruel. Unwilling to relinquish his self-proclaimed title, Jun offered to settle the feud like a real man: by staging a gruel-eating contest.

With a carton of cigarettes on the line, the men began wolfing down the oatmeal-like slop with the fervor of Luciano Pavarotti at an all-you-can-eat buffet.

Then it happened. Midway through his eighth bowel of gruel, Jun's intestines literally *exploded*. He died a short time later.

His horrified opponent was awarded the crown . . . and the cigarettes.

CHAPTER XII

KNUCKLEHEAD JOCKS

In Chicago, sports fans take their teams seriously.

So when the Green Bay Packers beat the Chicago Bears in a November 1995 gridiron match, fans of the Windy City's team took out their aggression on a Packers fan . . . by *duct-taping him to a stop sign*.

The unidentified man had been watching the game at Casey's Cabin Tavern in Fox Lake, Illinois. When the final score was announced, he made no secret of his support for the opposing team.

Outraged and intoxicated, a group of diehard Bears fans forcibly removed him from the bar, taped him to a stop sign on Illinois Highway 173, and hung a sign over his head that read, PACKERS FAN.

The victim opted not to press charges when police cut him loose a few hours later.

A golfer in the United Kingdom defeated his opponent in a close match after receiving some unexpected help from a sheep.

Peter Croke, forty-seven, was involved in an intense game at the Southerndown Golf Club near Porthcawl in Mid Glamorgan when he duffed a ball on the seventeenth fairway. The wayward golf ball missed the hole Croke was aiming for, but found another—in a sheep's rear end.

The startled sheep, who had been leisurely dining on the course's well-kept greens, was knocked forward and began running—all the while keeping the ball firmly lodged in its anus.

"I just could not believe it," Croke later told reporters. "I followed the sheep . . . and then it obligingly deposited the ball for me on a footpath thirty yards ahead."

Fortunately, the animal ran in the right direction. When the ball finally jarred loose, it landed thirty yards *closer* to the green. He had no problem dumping the ball into the cup with a follow-up putt.

"It would have been great if it had walked up to the pin and dropped the ball in the hole, but I cannot complain," Croke said.

Croke had no trouble defeating his opponent, John Maher, who screwed up *his* next shot because he couldn't stop laughing.

In Georgia, Atlanta Braves pitcher John Smoltz was treated for five-inch-long welts after he tried to iron his polo shirt while wearing it. "I've ironed that way five or six times," he said, "and never had it happen before."

In Hong Kong a Taoist philosopher and martial arts expert has spent his life mastering the art of lifting ponderous weights— with his *penis*.

In a demonstration to show off his incredible talent, forty-nine-year-old Chan Tze-tan dropped his pants and tied a sturdy, red rope around his penis and testicles. Then, after pulling the rope tight, he affixed the other end to a stack of weights totaling 159 kilograms. As an anxious audience of men—women weren't allowed in the demonstration—looked on, Tze-tan lifted the metal disks twelve centimeters off the ground, keeping them suspended for a good ten seconds before releasing them.

Tze-tan said he had been lifting weights with his penis since he was ten years old.

When a West Virginia man decided to take up hunting, he cleared off a wall in his home to make room for the various trophies he'd receive from his conquests.

But instead of bringing back the head of some unsuspecting animal, "John," the would-be hunter, returned from his first outing with a court summons.

Local police charged John with negligence and hunting without a license after he bagged the biggest game of all: another hunter.

A fellow hunter was perched in a tree, waiting for *his* latest trophy to come trotting by. When John spotted him, he cocked his rifle and fired, hitting his prey in the left testicle.

As police led John away he said, "I can't help it if he looks like a squirrel."

———

If you're serious about the game, golfing requires a great deal of concentration.

But a group of hackers in Florida apparently took their game *too* seriously. While golfing at the Boca Raton Municipal Golf Course in February 1996, the four men were concentrating so hard they didn't even notice an airplane heading right toward them.

Flight instructor Scott Slinko was teaching a student the ins and outs of aviation when his plane—the Piper Aero—began experiencing engine trouble. Not wanting to take any unnecessary risks, Slinko decided to make an emergency landing on the first fairway.

Fortunately, he was able to set the craft down without a hitch. Unfortunately, the gaggle of golfers was right in the plane's path.

"Everything would have been okay if those damn golfers would have moved out of the way," Slinko said. "We were coming down and they weren't moving."

So, to avoid running over the oblivious foursome, Slinko was forced to veer the plane to the right, smashing it into a palm tree. Both instructor and student were unharmed, but the Piper Aero was totaled.

One of the golfers—Irv Brown—fended off blame for the incident.

"Concentration—that's the name of the game. That's what Jack Nicklaus said," Brown told reporters. "We were concentrating."

————

A European TV show called *The World* was canceled after an appearance by a jock who called himself "Mr. Power Tool."

During a live broadcast, Mr. Power Tool dropped his pants and tied one end of a rope to his penis. After connecting the other end to a chair, the performer enticed a woman from the audience to sit on the chair as he dragged it across the stage.

And it all happened in full view of the cameras.

GRANDMOTHER OF EIGHT MAKES HOLE IN ONE

Talk about dedication—an amateur golfer finished a tournament in Brussels, Belgium, after being burdened with the worst handicap in the history of the sport: a heart attack.

Pedro Brugada, a well-known cardiologist in Brussels, was about to begin the final round of the competition when he collapsed facedown on the green. Another golfer—who also happened to be a doctor—discovered that Brugada's heart had stopped beating. He revived his opponent and summoned an ambulance, which whisked Brugada off to the nearest hospital.

When Brugada woke up in the emergency room about an hour later, he was perturbed that he didn't finish the tournament. So, as soon as the doctor's back was turned, the cardiologist ran out of the hospital, grabbed a cab, and hightailed it back to the golf course.

Ninety minutes later Brugada won the tournament.

―――――――

Here's *one* achievement you probably won't find on the back of Deion Sanders's trading card: the first-degree misdemeanor charge he picked up on a visit to Fort Myers, Florida.

In June 1996 the Dallas Cowboys superstar apparently had some time to kill while passing through the Southwest Florida International Airport. Remembering a pristine lake he'd spotted on the airport's property, he pulled out his fishing pole and made like Andy and Opie to the water's edge, eager to drop a line and relax in the Florida sunshine.

There was a flaw in his plan, however. The lake was restricted.

Whether he didn't see the warning signs or his quest for "the big one" clouded his judgment, the Lee County Port Authority didn't really care. They charged Sanders with trespassing.

"The only defense I have is that I'm sorry, but they were biting," Sanders said.

═══════════

Ever since he joined the New York Yankees in 1946, sports reporters could always count on Yogi Berra to spice up their otherwise routine stories with his colorful—not to mention non-sensical—quotes.

Although the baseball legend hung up his catcher's mitt back when Richard Nixon ran the country, Berra continues to confuse young sports fans with his mangled words of wisdom.

After accepting an honorary doctoral degree from Montclair State University in New Jersey, the most-quoted man in baseball offered these gems:

- "During the years ahead, when you come to the fork in the road, take it."
- "Don't always follow the crowd, because nobody goes there anymore. It's too crowded."

- "You can observe a lot by watching."
- "Remember that whatever you do in life, ninety percent of it is half mental."
- "Thank you, Montclair State University, for making this day necessary."

⸻

The date: May 12, 1996.

After years of sitting on their coolies watching the professionals do all the work, sports fans finally found an athletic event of their *own*: "the .5 Kilometer Race for the Motivationally Challenged."

More than a hundred armchair quarterbacks set their VCRs, hiked up their gym shorts over their bellies, and headed out to the event, which was held in Buffalo, New York. Fortunately, there was no need to rush—thoughtful organizers abandoned the traditional early morning starting time so the entrants could sleep in.

After congregating at three P.M., the participants "warmed up" by scarfing down sub sandwiches, doughnuts, and soda. Once every artery-hardening morsel had vanished, they were ready for action.

The "runners" were divided into four groups: Lazy Boys, Channel Surfers, Couch Potatoes, and Couch Kings. When the timekeeper finally mustered up enough energy to fire the starting pistol, the race—which some might liken to the "Tortoise and the Hare" fable, sans the hare—was finally under way.

Instead of customary water stations, the .5 kilometer course—about four city blocks—was peppered with beer stops, complete with couches, chicken wings, and free cigarettes.

Despite all the built-in handicaps, the predominantly male assemblage was taught yet another lesson by the opposite sex. Winning honors were bestowed upon two *women*—Patti Jo Calabrese and Roberta Schreiber—who tied for last place with times of 13 minutes 19 seconds.

CHAPTER XIII

KNUCKLEHEADS IN THE NUDE

The career of a New Jersey firefighter was cut short after he made the headline on the August 26, 1995, edition of the *Trentonian*: NUDE FIREMAN CHARGED IN BREAK-IN.

The incident occurred two days earlier in the home of John Parry, a wealthy psychologist who lived in a West Windsor, New Jersey, mansion known to locals as the "Castle." After hearing his doorbell ring at eight A.M., Parry came downstairs to find a stranger standing in his foyer. The intruder—thirty-year-old Jeff Sawsky—shook Parry's hand and greeted him as if the two were old friends.

"He just stepped right into the house and put his glasses and binoculars on the credenza, put his hat on the piano, pulled off his red T-shirt, and started for the stairs," Parry later told reporters.

About halfway up the elegant staircase the off-duty firefighter dropped his jeans and underwear before leaning over the railing to shake Parry's hand again. As soon as Sawsky was out of sight, Parry rushed to a phone and called 911.

When officers arrived, they burst into a locked bedroom and found Sawsky—completely naked—standing in the middle of the room, screaming. He bolted past the startled cops and locked himself in another bedroom across the hall.

By the time they broke down *that* door, Sawsky had worked himself into a complete frenzy. It took "several" policemen and a can of Mace to get him under control. After handcuffing him, police escorted the man outside, where they hosed him off to relieve him of the Mace.

Parry gave his statement and escorted the arresting officers to the door before checking on his wife, who was still holed up in the master bedroom.

She was still sound asleep, and didn't believe Parry's story until she saw it on the local news later that afternoon.

———

On May 6, 1995, a woman entered a home in Keyport, Long Island, climbed on top of the resident's kitchen table, and attempted to urinate in a fruit bowl.

After having no luck, she climbed back down and took off all her clothes.

The residents of the home said they didn't know the woman, but described her as "intoxicated."

———————

Ever since New York's famed Brooklyn Bridge opened on May 24, 1883, local police have seen their share of strange occurrences on the link between Manhattan and the former home of the Los Angeles Dodgers. But none as strange—or as coincidental—as what happened nearly 110 years later.

Just after five-thirty A.M. on May 8, 1993, a naked man disrupted early morning traffic when he ran onto the East River crossing screaming, "It's a beautiful day! It's a beautiful day!"

According to Joseph DePlasco, a spokesman for the New York City Department of Transportation, the unidentified man was attempting to run from Manhattan to Brooklyn in the center lane of the Brooklyn-bound side. Apparently, the stripped sprinter was too busy enjoying the day to pay attention to the irate motorists who were swerving around him. About halfway across the bridge the man did a little swerving of his own—and crossed over into the right-hand lane. He was hit by a car and died at the scene.

Considering the chaos that would result if the bridge was shut down during rush hour, responding officers kept their investigation short and traffic was back to normal sometime between six-thirty and seven A.M.

The respite was short-lived, however. At seven A.M. a Seattle woman noticed an open door on the bridge's west tower. So, doing what *any* curious tourist would do, she got out of her car and began scaling a cable that led to the unsecured opening.

After attempts to talk her down failed, four Emergency Service Unit workers followed her up the cable and eventually succeeded in bringing her down. The rescue operation resulted in a temporary closing of the bridge, causing a traffic jam that stretched thirty blocks on Brooklyn's Flatbush Avenue and several miles on the Brooklyn-Queens Expressway.

When questioned by police, the woman—thirty-one-year-old Karen Cole—insisted she hadn't ascended the cable with the intention of jumping; simply, she was curious as to what was behind the open door. As Cole was taken away, she admonished her rescuers for leaving the lofty entrance open and for not posting signs indicating the cables were off limits.

Cole was taken to Bellevue Hospital for observation, and a twenty-one-year-old Brooklyn resident later turned himself in for driving the car that struck the naked man. No charges were filed against either party.

"Did you know everything that happens on the Brooklyn Bridge happens in May?" DePlasco pointed out.

Forget the hood ornament. Police in Banning, California, arrested a twenty-three-year-old woman after they caught her standing through the sunroof of a speeding car—*completely naked*.

When questioned by authorities, the woman—Teresa Brantley—explained it "turns her on" when she feels the wind against her bare skin. Besides, since the car was being piloted by her cousin, she didn't feel she was in any danger.

Brantley's cousin—Wayne Hall—had a slightly better defense: He told officers he was speeding because he was "embarrassed" by the added pair of fog lights and he wanted to get home as soon as possible.

The cops booked Hall on suspicion of drunk driving. Brantley was charged with public intoxication and indecent exposure.

You'd think the residents of Vinton, Louisiana, had never seen a naked man. On August 19, 1993, the Vinton Police Department was flooded with calls from concerned citizens—all claiming to have spotted a "naked stranger" driving through their otherwise quiet community.

Soon after an all-points-bulletin was issued, an alert patrolman stopped a 1990 Pontiac Grand Am that matched the vehicle's description. Sure enough, when the driver emerged from the car, he was wearing nothing but a towel. But before the officer had a chance to question him, the man dove back into his vehicle and sped away.

The resulting chase ended with the Grand Am crashing into a tree. This time, however, the stunned policeman watched as twenty people climbed out of the car—all wearing nothing but their birthday suits.

"They didn't have a stitch of clothes on," Vinton Police Chief Dennis Drouillard said. "I mean, no socks, no underwear, no nothin'."

Although the car was totaled, the passengers—all members of the same family heading for a Pentecostal religious retreat in Florida—suffered only minor injuries.

"I guess when you're packed in that tight, there's not much room to move around," Drouillard explained.

The group of naked travelers, who ranged in age from one to sixty-five, included three pregnant women and five children. The children had been riding in the trunk.

At first investigators had a tough time sorting out the details of the ill-fated journey. "They didn't say much," Drouillard said. "They mainly got out and chanted religious sayings."

Finally, one of the passengers spilled the beans: The driver, Sammy Rodriguez, and his brother, Danny—two Pentecostal preachers from Floydada, Texas—believed the devil was after their entire family. To make matters worse, their presence put the entire population of Floydada in serious jeopardy.

"They made statements like the devil was after them and Floydada was going to be destroyed if they stayed here," Floydada Police Chief James Hale said.

So the Rodriguez brothers packed up their families and headed for an unidentified religious sanctuary in Florida. The group left Floydada in five cars, but were forced to abandon four of them as they broke down along the way.

Somewhere along the line all twenty members of the Rodriguez family stripped and threw their clothes onto the highway after realizing the devil had already possessed their garments.

Twenty-nine-year-old Sammy Rodriguez—the pastor of the Templo Getsemani Assembly of God Church in Floydada—was arrested and charged with endangering the lives of children, reckless driving, flight from an officer, and other offenses. The other nineteen were released.

At Rodriguez's hearing the judge told him, "I don't know what possessed you to do what you did, but I'm relying on the statement you were told to do so by some higher being."

Rodriguez answered, "It wasn't God, sir."

He was fined $650.

———

NJ JUDGE TO RULE ON NUDE BEACH

In Greenfield, Wisconsin, owners of the Classic Lanes bowling alley decided to jazz up their otherwise humdrum sport by throwing a little humor their customers' way: On the outside of their building they posted signs reading BOWL NAKED, BOWL FREE.

Obviously, no one took them up on their offer. The regular customers got a few chuckles and business went on as usual.

Until April 16, 1996, that is. That's the day twenty-one-year-old Scott Hughes strolled into the bowling alley, rented a pair of shoes, selected a ball, and *proceeded to take off his clothes.* As a cluster of women from a local church group watched in horror, Hughes went on to bowl a 225 game—wearing nothing but a cowboy hat and bowling shoes.

By the time Greenfield police arrived, the free-floppin' Hughes was already into his second game. Officers made him put his clothes back on and ordered the establishment's owners to take down the signs. No charges were filed.

———

Bribes. Beatings. Dishonesty. Police departments all over the country periodically find themselves knee-deep in some controversy or another. But in the summer of '95 a scandal involving naked police officers rocked law enforcement agencies in several cities *at the same time*—but none as hard as the NYPD.

The trouble began at a police convention in Washington, D.C. Shortly after the dedicated officers arrived at the gathering, tales of excessive drinking, setting off fire alarms, groping women, terrorizing hotel guests, and running around naked started trickling back to the New York press. A widely publicized photograph showed a clearly hammered cop struggling to maintain his equilibrium while balancing a stack of beer cans on his forehead.

"The conduct of several dozen New York City police officers has tarnished the reputation of this department in ways that it has never been tarnished before," Police Commissioner William Bratton said.

And the tarnish grew thicker and deeper as cops started talking and more stories made it to print. Washington police were looking into assault charges involving an officer from the NYPD. Another flatfoot was entangled in a theft case. And people at Washington's Hyatt Regency told stories of a New York cop who stripped off his clothes and slid nude down a beer-slicked escalator.

To make matters worse, more than one loose-lipped policeman came forward and told how the escalator-sliding cop—nicknamed "Naked Man" by his peers—made a habit out of baring it all in public.

"He has that reputation," an anonymous officer told one reporter.

Bratton, speaking to a group of supervisors, said he was deeply embarrassed by the incident, adding he was even "ashamed" when he realized he was wearing an NYPD sweatshirt at a recent summit with top law enforcement officials.

"Walking around the conference with my wife, walking around the city, the stares wounded us," Bratton said.

———————

Life for Santa Claus can't be *all* good tidings and Christmas cheer.

Just ask twenty-five-year-old Heather Jaehn. After spending more than four hours lodged in her chimney, the diminutive 100-pound woman gained a whole new respect for ol' St. Nick.

The harrowing incident happened on June 18, 1996, after Jaehn and her boyfriend returned to her El Cajon, California, home after a quiet evening out. Realizing she'd forgotten her keys, Jaehn did what *any* levelheaded adult would do under such circumstances: She scaled the side of her house, scampered across the roof, and slipped down the chimney.

"I guess she thought if she broke a window, it would cost too much to fix," Ed Jarrell, battalion chief for the El Cajon Fire Department, said. "She figured it'd be easier to go down the chimney. She's a pretty small woman, you know."

Her boyfriend, who had been circling the house in search of another way in, knew something was askew when he heard Jaehn's muffled cries for help. After several unsuccessful attempts to reach the woman through the top of the chimney, he somehow broke into the house and tried pulling her down through the fireplace. Still no luck.

After three nightmarish hours, he finally called for the assistance of El Cajon's bravest.

"She was stuck in there pretty good," Jarrell said, "and I'm sure it was getting pretty claustrophobic in there. [The boyfriend] really should've called us sooner."

Before they knew it, the couple's "quiet evening" had turned so chaotic, observers must've felt they were watching a sitcom worthy of Lucy and Desi's funniest gags. In addition to thirteen firefighters, Jaehn's living room was soon jam-packed with dozens of newspaper writers, TV reporters, and several camera crews.

Another hour passed before rescue workers were finally able to pry the flustered woman free of the chute's Herculean grip. Black-faced and completely covered with soot, Jaehn was mortified when she found scores of strangers—some with TV cameras—staring at her when she emerged from the fireplace.

Only it wasn't her blackened face they were staring at.

A wave of silence swept the room and several jaws dropped. Jaehn was topless. No shirt. No bra. Nothing.

"It certainly was a surprise," Jarrell said. "We had no idea what was coming. I mean, the cameras were there and everything."

The way Jaehn explained it, the warm June evening and stifling brick prison became too much for her to handle. So, in a maneuver that would've made the Great Houdini proud, she cooled down by somehow managing to wiggle out of her sweater.

"I don't think she had a bra on to begin with," Jarrell offered, anticipating the obvious follow-up question. "*That* wouldn't have been so easy to take off. There wasn't a lot of room for her to reach around her back."

Jaehn was rushed to the hospital, where she was treated for minor cuts and bruises. But not before she put on a shirt.

"She was actually pretty lucky," Jarrell said. "Looking back, I'm sure she thinks there were probably better ways to break into the house."

SOURCES

ABC Morning Show
ABC Wake-Up Call
The Advocate
The Arizona Republic
Asbury Park Press
Associated Press
The Bergen Record
Caribbean Delight
Chicago Tribune
The Cleveland Plain Dealer
Eastern Express
The Globe & Mail
Guyan Sunday Chronicle
The Hollywood Reporter
Keene Sentinel
  (New Hampshire)
Knight-Ridder Inc.
Mesa Tribune
The Miami Herald
The Morning Call
  (Allentown, Pa.)

New York Newsday
New York Daily News
New York Post
The New York Times
Penthouse
The People
The Philadelphia Inquirer
The Raleigh News & Observer
Reuters Press
Roanoke Times & World-News
St. George Spectrum (Utah)
St. Louis Post-Dispatch
San Antonio Express News
San Francisco Examiner
San Jose Mercury News
The Tampa Tribune
The Trentonian
United Press International
USA Today
The Wichita Eagle

About the Author

Essentially a vaudeville entertainer who refuses to believe that vaudeville is dead, JOHN "KATO" MACHAY spent his first few years of adulthood as a reporter and humor columnist, bouncing around a mélange of newspapers in Chicago and Phoenix. It was during that time that he developed an interest in offbeat stories about unlucky saps in unusual situations. He'd clip and save all the strange anecdotes he stumbled across, depositing them in a file folder labeled "Knuckleheads." After trading in his reporter's notebook for a pair of headphones, Machay found work at radio stations in Phoenix, Seattle, and New York, where he currently earns his keep as the executive producer and on-air personality with WPLJ's highly-rated "Scott & Todd Show."

He currently resides in Verona, New Jersey, with his wife and two small children.